SUPER SEARCHERS

GO TO SCHOOL

**Sharing Online Strategies with K–12
Students, Teachers, and Librarians**

Joyce Kasman Valenza

Edited by Reva Basch

CyberAge Books

Information Today, Inc.
Medford, New Jersey

First Printing, 2005

Super Searchers Go to School: Sharing Online Strategies with K–12 Students, Teachers, and Librarians
Copyright © 2005 by Joyce Kasman Valenza

Super Searchers, Volume XIII
A series edited by Reva Basch

Library of Congress Cataloging-in-Publication Data

Valenza, Joyce Kasman.
   Super searchers go to school : sharing online strategies with K–12 students, teachers, and librarians / Joyce Kasman Valenza ; edited by Reva Basch.
      p. cm -- (Super searchers ; v. 13)
   Includes bibliographical references and index.
   ISBN 0-910965-70-6
   1. Internet searching--Study and teaching. 2. Web search engines--Study and teaching. I. Basch, Reva. II. Title. III. Series.

   ZA4230.V35 2005
   025.04'071--dc22

                                      2005015058

Printed and bound in the United States of America

President and CEO: Thomas H. Hogan, Sr.
Editor-in-Chief and Publisher: John B. Bryans
Managing Editor: Amy M. Holmes
VP Graphics and Production: M. Heide Dengler
Cover Designer: Jacqueline Walter Crawford
Book Designer: Kara Mia Jalkowski
Copy Editor: Dorothy Pike
Proofreader: Pat Hadley-Miller
Indexer: Enid L. Zafran

To Dennis

About The Super Searchers Web Page

At the Information Today Web site, you will find *The Super Searchers Web Page*, featuring links to sites mentioned in this book. We periodically update the page, removing dead links and adding additional sites that may be useful to readers.

The Super Searchers Web Page is being made available as a bonus to readers of *Super Searchers Go to School* and other books in the Super Searchers series. To access the page, an Internet connection and Web browser are required. Go to:

www.infotoday.com/supersearchers

Contents

Foreword

Surviving the Information Jungle

For most of us who finished our formal educations before 1995, research was conducted in an Information Desert. Those five or ten sources required for a research paper were darned tough to find in our schools and even our public libraries. Teachers and librarians performed much the same role as that of any desert guide: helping the student locate scarce resources in the educational environment. Remember how happy you were to find that last, perhaps only partially relevant, magazine article that met the minimum number of sources required? I do—vividly.

We teachers and librarians were pretty good as desert guides. We taught kids to use the card catalog, the *Readers' Guide to Periodical Literature*, the vertical file, reference sources, and indices. We knew where to look for that hidden waterhole, patch of shade, or edible lizard. We could because we were taught these exact skills ourselves as students. Libraries didn't change much in the first nine decades of the 20th century.

Today's student, who has access to online sources of information, has been thrust into the Information Jungle. A quick search using Google alone can yield thousands of potential sources. And "free" Internet access by the common search engines is just one trail in this great tangle. Wandering slightly off the well-trod path, the searcher discovers subscription data-bases, the "invisible" Web, massive online union catalogs from which print materials can be interlibrary-loaned, newsgroups, digital multimedia collections, chat rooms, and e-mail contact with individuals. Now educators have the challenge of acting as jungle guides—helping learners to find, evaluate, and select resources of genuine value. With the number of resources now overwhelming rather than scarce, avoiding snakes, telling the good berries from the poisonous ones, keeping away from the quicksand, and finding a way out of the undergrowth are the "skills" we as teachers and librarians need to help our students rapidly acquire.

The challenge is that this change from desert guide to jungle guide has been so rapid that many educators have not had time to learn the skills of an Information Jungle guide. I don't remember being taught anything about Boolean logic, advanced search pages, or metasearches in my B.C. (Before Computers) library school classes. Yahoo! was a just a term of endearment for seventh graders, the library catalog was still a bunch of wooden boxes, and the arrangement of most reference sources could be mastered by quietly humming the alphabet song. I was trained to use a walking stick and map, not a machete and GPS!

Every aspect of doing research has been impacted by the Information Jungle closing in around us. Not only do today's learners need new search skills, but they also need to be able to do the following:

- Carefully articulate the problem to be solved or the question to be answered

- Effectively evaluate the reliability of the information found

- Use their research findings to develop original solutions to problems of personal relevance

- Use information technologies, such as multimedia presentations, Web pages, and digital video, to communicate the findings and conclusions of problem-based activities

- Develop assessment tools that help improve their information searching, evaluating, and communicating skills, and that encourage reflection on the efficacy of these activities

- Develop a love of researching, reading, problem solving, and learning

Thankfully, my friend and colleague Joyce Valenza has put this book together. Not only is she, herself, about the sharpest tracker in the Information Jungle, she has found other real experts who know their way through this techno-maze. Through these interviews, they teach us their methods, so we in turn can teach them to our students and teachers. H. Rider Haggard could not have created a group of more intrepid explorers. Sheena—I mean Joyce—thanks for doing this for all of us who not only have to preach life long learning, but practice it as well.

Information problem-solving skills are the most critical skills any school can teach its students. Savvy citizens will be using these skills throughout their lives. And the information necessary to intelligently select a community in which to live, a political candidate for whom to vote, a lawnmower to purchase, or a business proposal to accept will increasingly be harvested online.

Don your pith helmets, folks. Let's plunge into the Information Jungle's dangers and delights!

Doug Johnson
Mankato (MN) Area Public Schools
www.doug-johnson.com

Acknowledgments

Thanks to John Bryans, who searched the field of teacher librarians to find me for this project.

Thanks to wise series editor Reva Basch, for her expert skills of refining, de-duping, detecting jargon, clearing fuzzy queries, and searching through what often looked like very noisy results to find the good stuff.

Thanks to patient transcriber Patty Shannon, who captured every darn word (with precision and recall!), many of which we wished we had never said, typing and optimizing our pages right up to the last minute before her vacation.

Mega-thanks to Alice, David, Deb, Debbie, Frances, Kathy, Ken, Linda, Marjorie, Pam, Peter, Sue, and Doug, who generously allowed me to search their vast stores of knowledge to share some of their best results with many more potential users.

And although cell phones contributed hugely to domestic tranquility while I tied up the landline on this project, I am grateful to Dennis, Emily, and Matthew for tolerating my confusingly passionate conversations about stuff that hardly seemed as important as real life and dinner.

Introduction

In 1976, fresh out of library school, I landed an impressive first professional gig. Hired to lead a team of scientists from the Franklin Institute in creating an online database on carcinogen research for Stanford University, I was in absolute awe of the knowledge and expertise of my project partners. But it was *me*, a baby librarian, completely green, who was creating the controlled vocabulary and database structure that would allow medical researchers around the world to share and build on their discoveries and treatments.

This database supercharged the currency of information in an arena where sharing of knowledge could literally mean life or death. I recognized that, with this very primitive database, I was providing a targeted group of information seekers with great power. The librarians at the other end of our database, those who were helping scientists access the actual information for which we created structure, were making a similar difference. As a new librarian, I recognized that databases *rocked*! There was a certain sexiness about electronic information retrieval. Sometime around 1986, I retooled and learned how to search the Dialog databases, dialing up via acoustic coupler. Dialog's overstuffed notebooks of "blue pages" opened a world of specialized searching. When I selected the right databases from among the pages of documentation and constructed an elegant search statement, I was shocked by my new powers to pull information from a searching universe way beyond my meager stacks. When I'd try to discuss my new powers over dinner with family or friends, their excitement was underwhelming. Around 1996, I was singing the praises and the powers of telnet and gopher to students and friends who could care less. Although they smiled indulgently, few of my teacher colleagues, and even fewer of my students, found ASCII interfaces sexy. Then, suddenly, the Web in all its "GUI-ness" came to school. It grabbed us all with its beauty, its friendliness, and its powers. *That* was sexy. Searching was not just for librarians anymore. Suddenly everyone was searching.

Today, searchers of all shapes and sizes—scientists, scholars, consumers, kids—have, whether they realize it or not, great power. Everyone is an end-user. But not every end-user is equally skilled or prepared. Not every searcher has a searcher's mindset, the kind of mindset many of us developed as we built strategies using controlled vocabularies, scanned through those notebooks of blue pages, and refined our queries, building "ss" command lines while watching the clock tick off costly online time.

Some end-users know how to make the tools of searching sing for them; others have not a clue that they could fine-tune their searches—or that they should care.

IT'S NOT CALCULUS AND YET ...

Searching is a life skill. *Which car or stereo should I buy? Which college should I choose? Which book should I read next? Is this doctor adequately prepared to diagnose my condition or perform my surgery? How can I sell this idea to my boss? How can I convince the board to accept my proposal? For whom should I vote?* We are always seeking information. Information helps us reach conclusions, make important life choices, and communicate more effectively. Those who can locate the good stuff and use it well have a real advantage.

Today's students are the first generation of learners to grow up with true information bounty, diversity, and, yes, overload. They may not remember a time before e-mail and graphic user interfaces. And they may be falsely confident about their ability to navigate, evaluate, and communicate effectively in the vast information landscape they consider their own turf.

Librarians may worry that Web users settle for "good enough" information, often ignoring the very best of the materials available to them. Recent research, such as Pew Data Memo on Search Engines [142, see Appendix] and the 2003 OCLC Environmental Scan [138] indicates, "that information consumers are, by and large, satisfied with the quality of the information they find on the Web."

But *I* will not accept that my students know enough, nor will I allow them to stop learning. Math teachers don't stop their instruction after students learn to add, subtract, multiply, and divide. I expect my students to be knowledgeable and effective information users.

This is a landscape in which we all must be continual learners. I have a hunch that few students realize how much they still have to learn, how they might yet improve their research strategies in preparation for the worlds of college, work, and citizenship. If students are to grow to be effective adult consumers of information, they will need to develop a skill set known as information fluency, to be able to efficiently locate, evaluate, analyze, synthesize, and communicate information. And they will need teachers and librarians capable of staying far ahead of the curve.

Smart students are not always good researchers. Students who master such challenges as algebra and calculus, students who can analyze the great and thorny works of literature, are not necessarily good searchers. Why not?

- A know-it-all sense of self-efficacy may present barriers to learning and to seeking the best stuff. The turf on which we ask students to perform academically is the very same turf our students use as their playgrounds and entertainment venues. The channel they regularly use for casual communication is the same channel we now expect them to use for formal academic communication and research. Though we celebrate student familiarity with this landscape, their transfer of entertainment habits to more serious academic enterprises presents problems. Students have high expectations for speed and immediate response in their casual searching and communication, and those expectations are not necessarily reasonable in research.

The search process is messy, confusing, challenging, and time-intensive.

• The Internet has transformed research into a largely independent pursuit. Gone may be the chat a parent would conduct during the car ride to the library. Gone may be the in-person "reference interview," as librarians call it, where an information professional intervenes to help a student assess a problem, focus a topic, suggest keywords, point to a critical book, or recommend the best index or database in which to begin a search. The student researcher is most often in his or her own room, without any chance of adult intervention, happily diverted by instant messages and e-mail. Student independence is something we promote and can celebrate at many stages in the research process, but there are points where adult interaction is critical. Even the brightest of our 17-year-olds don't know what they don't know—the keywords associated with a specialized field, the historical context for an event, the seminal works or classics in a particular area of knowledge.

• Although teacher-librarians learn searching skills in pre-service programs, most classroom teachers do not. Well-intentioned though they might be, a large number of educators approach searching without refined knowledge of how to help their students move the best items up to the top of a result list, how to evaluate a "works cited" page with savvy, how to guide learners to the appropriate search-tool options, or how to learn about the developmentally appropriate databases for helping students prepare for the research tasks they will face. And classroom teachers may not be aware that they have knowledgeable partners, teacher-librarians who will help them every step of the way, in planning, implementing, and assessing inquiry-driven activities for learners. Parents, too, may not be aware of the help a teacher-librarian can offer, K–12, in guiding them through their students' information-seeking and-using experience.

WHAT DOES AN INFO-FLUENT STUDENT LOOK LIKE?

As I conducted interviews with my esteemed colleagues, I recognized that what we were really talking about was preparing the next generation to participate in emerging information landscapes. I imagined what, exactly, we would be looking for as students left the realm of our immediate influence.

My ideal exiting senior possessed both searching knowledge and searching *attitude*. Good researchers not only have skills, they exhibit a set of habits and behaviors that promote success. In terms of cognitive abilities, the information-fluent student:

- *Knows what he or she is looking for.* It may take some messing around at first, but the info-fluent student has a clue about the area he or she is researching. This may mean doing some background reading before conducting any serious searching. Any thesis-based project requires significant reading and refining before a student can move from topic to question to thesis. The info-fluent student learns to disregard material that does not further the question or support the thesis.

- *Realizes he or she has search choices.* Google [15] rocks, but it is not the only band in town and is not always the best place to start. Although a student may not recognize the names of more than two or three search tools, the info-fluent student knows that there are clusters or genres of such tools—search engines, subject directories, subscription databases, subject-specialized portals, news, reference, media tools, and so on—and that certain tools are more effective for certain tasks. He or she recognizes that these clusters exist and may ask for help finding them.

Teachers may opt to create a search-tool page like mine [156], or link to Debbie Abilock's Choose the Best Search for Your Information Need [92], or Laura Cohen's How to Choose a Search Engine or Directory [93].

- *Recognizes research holes.* The info-fluent student who is immersed in a topic begins to note the names of the experts and the important books that people cite repeatedly. He or she examines the bibliographies of others, knowing that overlooking important people, sources, and concepts would constitute holes in his or her research.

- *Knows basic strategies for evaluating sources.* The info-fluent student knows that authors' credentials are important, that any cited source ought to be defendable in terms of relevance, timeliness, bias, credibility, accuracy, and reliability. He or she knows that free hosting services like AOL Members [85] or Geocities [105] should raise red flags on result lists and are likely to raise red flags on "works cited" pages. Reliable authors don't usually rely on free services with their ubiquitous advertising. Instead, these authors are affiliated with and hosted by museums, universities, and other respected institutions. The info-fluent student realizes that some results are sponsored and is suspicious of such results.

- *Recognizes that searching is an interactive, recursive process.* I once asked a student what he did when he hadn't gotten the results he'd hoped for. He responded, "I go to another search engine and do exactly the same thing." When things don't go well, info-fluent students consider the cause and refine their search strategies. They know a tip or help sheet is readily available within most search tools. They examine and mine their result lists for alternate ideas, words, and phrases.

- *Knows that there are a variety of ways to search—keyword, subject/topic, and field searching.* This basic concept may not be obvious to a user who does not move beyond Google's front screen. Most subscription databases offer the obvious choice of a topic browse or a keyword search. Advanced search screens often offer opportunities to filter by field, date, or file type, as well as opportunities to easily use Boolean strategies.

- *Knows how to think about a query.* Natural language searching, asking a search box questions as if you were engaging in regular conversation, does not give a searcher much power. When a student learns how to construct a query, he or she knows how to formally pose a question to a search box, making maximum use of its syntax or special language.

- *Knows when quality matters.* Do I ever do sloppy Google searches? You bet—when I am checking on spelling or getting a broad idea of what's out there. But when I know it matters, I create thoughtful queries. I visit specialized databases. I figure out who wrote the documents that I find and where they were originally published.

But these cognitive abilities won't stick unless they are supported by attitudes and behaviors—by habits of mind. Hence, the information-fluent student also:

- *Has a sense of inquiry.* The info-fluent student is curious and develops exploratory questions out of that curiosity.

- *Thinks creatively about words.* He or she is able to envision a "dream document" and what significant words and phrases that document might contain, what synonyms might effectively replace those words that did not do the job at first.

- *Manages time effectively.* The info-fluent student does not back himself into a time crisis. He or she understands that good research takes time, that the process is recursive. It's all about refining, organizing, analyzing, drafting, concluding—about going back.

- *Has conceptual tools for organizing the materials he or she gathers as well as tools for designing the final product.* The info-fluent student continually looks for information patterns. What buckets does this information fit into? Does it look like a comparison? A chronology? A thesis? A debate? What type of presentation is likely to be most effective?

- *Is persistent and fussy.* The info-fluent student does not settle for "good enough" information. He or she recognizes that the first page of a result list may not contain the best stuff, and is willing to think about how a search may be improved, to refine strategies, to try another search tool. At times this may mean seeking full text when it is not easily available. If all that appears in a database is an abstract, and that abstract is "killer," the info-fluent student will seek the complete article, even if it means getting up and going to a library, checking another database, initiating interlibrary loan, visiting a bookstore, or locating a collection of e-books.

- *Recognizes when he or she might benefit from consulting an information professional.* The info-fluent student can put aside any sense of technological arrogance to ask for help. His or her question might have nothing to do with technology. It might, perhaps, involve brainstorming alternate keywords. It may be about potential sources beyond the free Web, about the particular experts in a specialized field, or about the unique vocabulary of a new area of knowledge.

BUT WHAT ABOUT US?

We are the first generation of teachers, librarians, and parents who have had to teach and guide in a Web-based infoscape. It is critical that we catch and equip this first generation of computer-savvy students with the knowledge and habits of mind they need. But no long-established pedagogy guides us. No tested and true scope and sequence helps us plan and articulate instruction from grade to grade. Teaching in and about an environment that is in constant flux is like shooting at a swiftly moving target, but it can be thrilling.

Effective K–12 teachers and librarians, like those I interview here, are catching this current generation of Web learners. These Super Searchers, and their many colleagues out in the trenches, help young people become savvy searchers and information users—help them understand when "good enough" information is simply *not* good enough. They are teaching on two fronts. In addition to teaching traditional learners, they are working with a largely unschooled population of fellow educators and administrators. This is a critical audience for instruction. Their partner educators must be reached and trained if students are to value these information skills.

Although we expect our students to master the complexities of higher-level math and to read and analyze great literature, we often accept low quality and limited effort and energy in students' searching for and processing of information. In many schools we tolerate, forgive, and neglect to assess student lack of scholarship in this arena. How can we improve teacher awareness of critical information skills, convincing them to set high expectations for information fluency? How do we spread the gospel of information fluency across the curriculum? How and when do we teach and assess these sophisticated concepts and thinking skills? How do we get past students' sense of self-efficacy while respecting their abilities? How can educators and librarians intrude respectfully when research becomes a largely self-service pursuit? What are the developmental issues in teaching searching? What does best practice look like? How can we motivate learners to care about improving their searching skills? How can we motivate them to care about selecting high-quality resources? And how can we engage the entire learning community—classroom teachers, administrators, and parents—in these efforts?

My Super Searcher colleagues explore these questions and propose some solutions. What separates the Super Searchers here from those in the other books in this series [202] is that, in addition to performing the magic necessary to get information into the hands of others, these educators and educator-librarians are responsible for and committed to sharing the secrets of their magic with the "clients" they serve, committed to passing their knowledge on. Their pedagogical and public relations strategies are as varied as the teaching styles you will find in any K–12 school district. Teachers, librarians, and parents can learn from these professionals, their stories of effective strategies, and the steps and missteps they've made.

Each of our K–12 Super Searchers shares a slightly different approach for working with learners. Debbie Abilock talks about tools for critical thinking and applies a constructivist model to her strategies with very young learners. Alice Yucht's and Deb Logan's stories and metaphors help learners develop schema, mental pictures of the Web. Kathy Schrock shares her experiences and deep Web wisdom, and encourages us to get students to step back from their workstations and *think*. Frances Jacobson Harris works with learners on understanding what goes on inside databases and search tools. David Barr studies student search knowledge, skills, and attitudes, and designs interfaces to guide them through the problems they encounter. Business teacher Sue Fox describes the importance of skilled searching in her classroom program. Marjorie Pappas urges us to consider the importance of information-processing models in student learning. Linda Joseph focuses on the importance of evaluation. Peter Milbury reminds librarians and educators of the guidance that virtual libraries and pathfinders can provide. Pam Berger reminds us we are merely at the tip of the iceberg as we attempt to interpret this medium in educationally sound ways for 21st century learners.

Each of our contributors offers search tips in a unique format, some terse, some more expansive, depending on the audiences they reach and their personal teaching styles. Some responded with tips for students, some for teachers, others for fellow librarians or a combination of two or all three. I have included the tips as I received them, in all their variety, for their own charm and for the sense of possibility, personality, and style they contribute.

As I interviewed, my greatest challenge was to keep my own ideas out of my interviewees' way. Even though I was asking the questions, I had way too much to say, as a practitioner myself, about everything. This introduction is my opportunity to hold forth a bit, so I'll end with my own tips for what teachers and librarians can do to encourage better information seeking and use:

- *Create research challenges.* Eliminate reports that merely ask for recall. That sort of work—report on a state or president or planet—is far too easily copied and printed. Ask students instead to explore provocative questions, to compare, analyze, evaluate, and invent, rather than paraphrase.

- *Evaluate students' "works cited" lists.* Value variety. Value research energy. On the high school level, reward the use of scholarly sources. On other levels, reward the use of quality sources from reliable databases and journals. Learn to recognize suspicious URLs. Any mention of Google, Yahoo! [43], or AltaVista [3] should send a message that the student is referencing the index, not the original source, and has likely avoided energetic research. Did the student make any attempt to balance resources among books, journals, and general Web sites? Did he or she attempt to balance points of view? Be aware, when you look for balance, that a book is a book, whether it appears as an e-book in netLibrary or a physical volume from the stacks. An article from *National Geographic* is a magazine article, whether it comes from the shelves or an online database.

- *Scaffold.* Help your students develop organizers for data collection and restructuring. A Venn diagram or a matrix will help students collect data for comparing and contrasting. A timeline or flowchart may aid in the analysis of an historic event. A concept map will help students as they brainstorm subheadings or arguments supporting a thesis.

- *Create online pathfinders.* Pathfinders are blueprints for student research. Focused on a specific project or a particular curriculum, they create a kind of self-service intervention, respecting students' independence while guiding them through the process. Pathfinders may suggest keywords, databases, specialized search engines, directories, call numbers, and multimedia resources, any particular advice necessary for success on a specific project. Project rubrics should heavily value the suggestions of the pathfinder. (See pathfinder examples at my Virtual Library.)

- *Create an appropriate search-tool page on your Web site for general student research.* Do you want students to start with Google? EBSCOhost [53]? Gale Literature Resource Center [61]? ProQuest Historical Newspapers [68]? KidsClick! [23]? Facts on File [57]? World Book [74]? Let them know; make these tools no more than a mouse click or two away. Link students to the more powerful advanced search screens of the search engines you'd like them to use.

- *Ask students to annotate their works cited lists.* Annotations are metacognitive activities that force and value critical thinking and careful selection. In an annotation, students should consider authors' credentials, relevance of the source to their project, how it compared to other sources, and how it informed their knowledge. Create criteria for evaluating annotations and assess them as student projects.

- *Use formative or in-process assessments to check students' progress as they research.* Collect organizers, outlines, source cards, note cards, tentative thesis statements, and preliminary "works consulted" pages. If you assess only at the end, it's too late. Assessing the process throughout the project has the greatest learning value.

- *Keep up as the search environment continues to evolve*—as Google promises to help academic libraries digitize their holdings and as federated searching improves to help students cut across their toolkits.

Ultimately, searching is about problem solving and decision making. It is about learning to learn. We will always be seeking, evaluating, analyzing, and using information.

In this dynamic digital-information landscape even the most super of our Super Searchers must keep improving their powers. I hope that the wisdom of the Super Searchers you meet here will inspire you to hone your own skills and to share new skills with others, especially the students in your life. As you continue to refine your own searches I wish you many relevant results.

Pam Berger

The Information Searcher— Teaching Teachers and Librarians to Search

Currently a library and educational technology consultant and grant writer, Pam Berger was a high school librarian for 14 years. She is editor and publisher of the quarterly newsletter *Information Searcher* [169, see Appendix] and InfoSearcher.com, and is the author of *Internet for Active Learners: Curriculum-Based Strategies for K–12* [180] and *21st Century Strategies for Strengthening Your School Library Program* [181]. Pam was the chair and a founding member of the American Association of School Librarians' national technology initiative, ICONnect.

pberger@infosearcher.com
www.infosearcher.com

We met back in 1995. You had just published *CD-ROM for Schools*. I'll bet you've had some fun observing the changes in the information landscape.

The changes have been dramatic. The development of the Internet and the Web has brought searching directly to the end-user in a way that we never dreamed of back then. In 1993 I was working in Armonk, New York, as a high school librarian, and I received a grant from the New York State Department of Education to research the educational impact of using Internet resources with advanced biology and history classes. It was before the Web, even before gopher; we were using UNIX commands. Teachers were very intimated by the process, and so was I, for that matter.

That was one of the reasons CD-ROM was so popular; it was manageable and available to everyone. There was very little information online and what was there was difficult to locate. The only truly relevant information for schools was on commercial databases such as Dialog [52]. And although librarians could effectively search Dialog with its controlled vocabulary and Boolean search operators, it was difficult for most teachers and students. Internet searching didn't truly become mainstream until the introduction of Google [15] around 1998. It opened up the floodgates for end-user searching. Everybody searches the Internet directly for information—teachers, students, administrators. Everyday, millions of times a day, people Google. We experienced a major shift in searching behavior from 1995 to 2004. Maybe it should be called the Decade of the End-User.

I remember that shift clearly. But I am concerned that even experienced end-users have a rather naive understanding of searching.

I agree, and the latest research backs that up. A survey by the Pew Foundation, part of the Pew Internet & American Life Project [142], found that 84 percent of online Americans have used search engines and that, on any given day, more than half of those using the Internet use search engines. What I found startling was the level of confidence that the average user has the ability to locate relevant information on the Internet. Some 87 percent of search engine users say they find information they want most of the time. More than 90 percent of searchers express confidence in their skills as searchers, and more than half say they are "very confident" that they can accomplish what they want when they perform an online search. And what's more amazing is that more than two-thirds, 68 percent, of search engine users say they consider search engines a fair and unbiased source of information—when it is estimated that

40 percent to 45 percent of searches include sponsored results. Searchers are finding *something* when they search, but I'm not sure it's the best "something" they can find. And I don't believe they are evaluating what they find. I think it is safe to say that the average user doesn't understand how search engines work or the differences among them.

By differences, you mean special features and specialized search engines?

Yes, I mentioned earlier that the last decade could have been called the Decade of the End-User. Well, we are now entering the Decade of the Search Engine. Over the past 10 years, we enticed the end-user into searching, and we added enough good information to the Internet to make them *want* to search. Now we need to make the search engines more effective. When I read comments from search engine developers and other people in the search engine industry, they talk about how to make their search engines more intuitive, more specialized, and more localized. Some of these specialized sites and unique features already exist, but students and teachers don't know about them.

Any tips for how to spread the word, Pam?

We should begin with rethinking our approach. We have to teach search engines as a strategy rather than a tactical approach. Based on the Pew findings and our own first-hand experience, we know that our students believe they know how to search. We must acknowledge their skill at searching, and at the same time provoke or challenge them to move to a higher level, to a problem solving or strategy level.

I recently heard an analogy comparing online searching to a chess game. There are two types of chess players. The tactical player reacts to every play as it comes along. Strategy plays no role in this approach. At each turn, he or she looks at the board and makes what appears to be the best move. But the strategic player looks at the big picture and explores the possible impact of all of his or her opponent's future moves. The strategist moves on to competitive chess.

Kids search on the tactical level, and that has to change. They need to understand the search process within the larger picture of inquiry, and develop strategies: What information do I need? Is a search engine the best way to find it? Based on my information need, which search engine will be most effective? Which ones have added value to support my search process? To be a strategist you need to develop a mental model and know what the information landscape looks like and what specialized search engines, such as KartOO [22] or Vivisimo [39], are available.

I like Vivisimo too. I just tried KillerInfo.com [24]. It's similar in its clustering features and in some cases the clusters appear more logical. Those clusters are never going to be perfect.

No, but they do offer an added value. Clustering helps kids understand what they have found by transforming long lists of search results into categorized information. Anything that leads students to organize is helpful.

Laura Cohen in Albany [94] labels the use of these clusters "horizontal searching." When I use the term with students they get it almost instantly. They're very familiar with vertical result lists. Google, for instance, forces you to scroll down in the results list, and sometimes the killer result is 10 pages down. But if you're searching horizontally and you bring these results up in your clusters, you might actually discover Google's result number 500 on the first search screen in a cluster, and you might also recognize the relevance of a particular cluster to your work. This horizontal

versus vertical approach seems to work as a kid-friendly concept.

I agree; it's very powerful and practical. Vivisimo isn't alone, of course, in offering clustering. Other sites such as Mooter.com [27], based in Australia, and Grokker [17], by the folks at Groxis in California, feature the technology, though in a significantly different way. Both of them display the clusters as diagrams that resemble astronomical charts, rather than mere text lists.

Librarians ought to keep their eyes on emerging changes in search engines, and think about how and why unique features like these can support their students in becoming effective searchers. A search engine like Topix.net [37] based in Palo Alto, features news from more than 6,000 sources such as newspapers, magazines, and government agencies. Users can search the site for news related to an individual town by typing in the ZIP code. Students can narrow the search for news on their hometown.

What other search engines are you watching?

Eurekster [9], based in San Francisco, takes an entirely different path to improve search quality. It relies on personalization and customization, technologies that some of the major engines are also exploring. The idea is to skew results based on past user behavior. The more often a user clicks on a particular Web site, the higher it will appear in subsequent searches for similar queries. But personalization on Eurekster doesn't stop there. Users can also elect to have their friends' search behavior influence their own results. It's a variation of social networking, the popular online phenomenon you see in such sites as Friendster [13]. As with social networking, users and their friends must register on Eurekster to get the full benefit of the personalization technology.

I mentioned Mooter earlier. It does not present results as a list; instead it offers a "nodal map," which groups results by themes. Grokker uses a graphical interface, like KartOO. We're just beginning to see where the Web is taking us, not just in terms of accessing information through searching, but also in terms of how we interact and how we create information. The Web is a transformative medium, and we're just beginning to understand that.

Transformative? Because of its potential as a medium for two-way communication?

Yes. It's not just about searching or merely downloading information. The Web is the first technology that makes user-to-user communication a reality. Newspapers offer letters to the editor, radio shows provide call-in opportunities for listeners, and TV... well, I guess you could point to talk shows. But with the Web, it's true interactivity. I think this generation of kids is the first to embrace the Web in a truly interactive way. Think about how many kids you know are into IM, instant messaging. This generation is perpetually hooked up; their use of the Web is seamless. Because of this seamlessness, students are constantly multitasking. Adult behavior is different. Adults log on and off the Web; they don't stay connected for days. Even when they leave their desks, college students instant-message, "be back in two seconds" or "gone for coffee." I find that fascinating. We tend to turn computers on and off, to start and stop. We still separate the various things we do online, while kids view the Web more holistically. They're also the first group to embrace blogging.

Yes, my daughter and her friends are just out of college and scattered all over the world. They now keep up with each other's lives through their blogs. I am so impressed with their dedication to this journaling. Do you notice any kind of

dissonance, Pam, when we try to put a pedagogy around something so ubiquitous?

Absolutely, you can feel the tension. Searchers want independence. However, there is still a tremendous need for librarians to intercede, but perhaps in a different way than we have been doing. We need to stand back and look at the searching environment and the users' expectations. We need to look at how information is packaged, how we search for it, how we interact with it, and then adapt our teaching strategies. The 2003 OCLC Environmental Scan [138] helped me to better understand the users' perspective, especially the average person's learning preferences. The trends that ring true to my experience are searchers' independence in information gathering, their satisfaction with their own searching skills and results, their expectation of interactivity and collaboration, and their desire for personalization. We need to address these factors as we develop units with teachers, design our library Web sites, and work with students. They might want to search without help, but they will need assistance in placing the results in a context they can understand. Collaborative groups, interactive library Web sites, pathfinders, and student reflection blogs are all strategies we can use to support students. We also need to look at the kinds of research assignments we are giving students.

Are you talking about changing the questions, the types of challenges we present to students?

Exactly. If we pose more inquiry-based research instead of topic research, which just asks kids to locate and copy information, students will naturally start posing questions and some of those questions will center on how to effectively search and evaluate information. In Barbara Stripling's Inquiry Process [209], the stages are Connect, Wonder, Investigate, Construct, Express, and Reflect.

Searching is, of course, used in the Investigation phase, but it can also be introduced in the Connect phase to help students to gain background knowledge and engage in the process. In the Reflection phase, they reflect on what they have learned but also on the inquiry process they have experienced. Part of that reflection is looking back at their search strategies and thinking about what they have learned and what they can add to their mental models of the information landscape.

Searching is a recursive activity. It is problem solving. It supports inquiry. What we really need to do is help students continuously develop more sophisticated mental models of the information environment, of which the constantly changing Internet is a huge part.

How do we best do that? What have you seen that works?

An instructional strategy that I have found effective and fun is Mind Mapping [130], which was invented by Tony Buzan, an author and creativity consultant. It's a powerful graphic technique. It is described as an expression of "radiant" thinking, meaning to spread or move in directions, or from a given center. It can be used to brainstorm and to graphically display information. It consists of a central word or concept in which you draw the five to ten main ideas that relate to that word. Each of the child-words has five to ten main ideas that relate to it. Although Buzan designed the technique to help facilitate the creative process, it has great application anywhere you need to organize your thoughts and tie together the two sides of your brain. The left side of our brain is where the analytical, logical component of our thinking process originates, while the right side is where ideas flow in the form of pictures and concepts. Buzan sought to find a method of conceptualizing ideas or planning work in which he could utilize the whole brain. Mind Mapping takes advantage of both, since it has you use text along with phrases, arrows, symbols, drawings, and so on.

I've used this technique, having students create Mind Maps of their search process by starting with a central symbol that depicts an essential question, and brainstorming the possible types of information sources. It helps me understand their mental models of information seeking, and it helps them organize their approach to searching and be more reflective. I'm writing an article for my newsletter on this approach, and there is information on my Web site about creating Mind Maps.

Can you discuss your newsletter a bit? I'm a big fan.

I try to keep *Information Searcher* focused on practical information, strategies, and tips that librarians can implement in their practice the next day or week and can share with teachers. The writers are primarily practicing school librarians, so they have a pulse on what's needed. I travel a lot in my consulting, working with school districts, public libraries, state associations and universities, and giving presentations. I get to meet and talk with a large cross-section of educators who, through sharing their experiences, help me better understand kids' searching behaviors and how we can best help them to be effective searchers. I try to translate all that into practical articles in my newsletter. I also facilitate a one-hour monthly session in Tapped In [159], an online collaborative environment for educators, called Web Tools. We collaboratively look at Web-based tools that support inquiry learning, and search engines are among the tools we investigate.

When you look five years down the search engine road, what does Pam Berger see?

Some of the hot trends we are looking at now are personalization and social networking. Personalized search engines collect information about the subjects that interest you; they know that you are interested in computers, not fruit, when you type "apple." Google Labs [16] has a version of this available. Social networking is currently represented by Web sites like Friendster.com and Meetup.com [26], which enable strangers to meet online with profiles of their interests and activities acting as bait for like-minded people. Search engines are picking up on this concept and are developing features that tweak the relevancy ratings of results according to the recent search queries of a user's friends. Eurekster allows searchers to create Info Nations. An Info Nation is a search engine focused around a particular topic, set up and governed by the people that use it. The idea is that personalization, social networking, and localized searching will retrieve more personally relevant sites, faster. I'll be interested in seeing if they make their way into mainstream searching and what impact they'll have on students' searching behavior. When did you say you were planning the update for this book?

Super Searcher Power Tips

➤ Run your search on different search engines and compare the results. Don't assume all search engines are the same.

➤ Don't assume that the large, general search engines are always the best. Consider a specialized index such as FindLaw [12], a database on legal code and case law, or Topix.net for local news.

➤ Learn to use a wildcard (often an asterisk) when searching, to find variations of words or word fragments.

➤ Beware of terms with double meaning. "Chicks" can pull up graphics of a scantily dressed woman, in addition to information on chicken hatching; "Spiders" can be computer programs used by search engines, or eight-legged araneae. Search engines like Vivisimo that cluster the results will help you in this area.

➤ Each search engine is different. Decide on your favorite and learn its nuances in depth. You'll be amazed what you can do with Google!

➤ If it is not clearly evident why a search engine retrieved a document, use your browser's Find button to search for your term in context on the page.

➤ Understand what you are looking for and know some of the terminology associated with your target topic. The broader and more ill-defined your search query, the more extraneous information you will find. You will learn about your subject as you search, but it's best to start with some basic background information so you can narrow down, increase your precision, and target the needed information.

➤ Check SearchEngineWatch.com [150] for the latest analysis and news about search engines. Read the "Search Engine Math" article for good search tips.

➤ Subscribe to the *Information Searcher* newsletter!

Debbie Abilock

The Importance of Messing Around and Clumping (Teaching Our Youngest Searchers)

Debbie Abilock is the editor of *Knowledge Quest* [170, see Appendix], the journal of the American Association of School Librarians [75]. She has more than 25 years experience in education as a teacher-librarian, school administrator, curriculum coordinator, and director of a unified library and technology department. She consults, writes, and speaks on issues of curriculum design, technology integration, and the teaching of new literacies. Abilock is co-founder of NoodleTools, a suite of Web-based interactive tools designed to aid students and professionals with online research.

debbie@noodletools.com
www.noodletools.com

You and I have been in the field quite a while. Initially, how did the Internet affect the way you approached learning?

We put the Internet into my school in 1992, so I did a lot of teaching around the command line. It was before Netscape; there was no graphical interface. We were telneting, using FTP, gopher, all those text-based applications. We also taught kids Dialog [52] searching.

At that grade level, that must have been a challenge.

We taught K–8 by teaching alongside their teachers. Even back then we were doing professional development around the Internet. We got a huge grant to train teachers and librarians. But because there was no graphical interface, it was pretty difficult. We discovered some interesting things. We found that teachers and students responded best to e-mail, because it was the most like what they were doing offline. It was like letter writing; the print analogy was there. The most difficult concepts to teach were things like FTP, because there was no print analogy to any of that. "Teaching the Internet" seemed like a huge task.

But when it all changed, when we moved to the graphical interface, it was as if something that I'd always found sexy suddenly became sexy to the rest of the world. Before, it was critical to teach syntax and commands. But when that change occurred, the end-user no longer saw the importance of any of that.

What the Web—the graphical user interface (GUI) to the Internet—did was to send a visual message that this was something that normal people could do. The command line interface sent a message that normal people couldn't do it. The visual metaphor of a GUI was an invitation to learn, and there was a growing demand to learn how to search, what to look for, and how to make sense of it.

Most of the teaching I did at the beginning of Netscape was very straightforward, simply putting in a single word or a couple of words—remember, I work with young kids—on the search line, and then looking at the results. It was never about the search; it was much more about looking at the results of the search and then thinking about how we could modify.

What I'm hearing is that you were reacting rather than planning.

That's right. It's similar to Piaget's messing-around stage. As learners we are all messing around, trying to figure out what happens if we do this, how does this impact that. We can't just hand inert knowledge to students, stuffing them with facts or routines like intellectual sausages. All learners manipulate objects, try to represent abstract concepts in language, and make intuitive and logical judgments as they go through a process of intellectual experimentation. At the same time that we're valuing our students' discovery process, we're also on the lookout to mediate their learning.

In those days I didn't do a lot of conceptual stuff. I didn't try to teach kids Dialog search strategies. However, Dialog had a couple of things that were very helpful as we began to search the Internet. Remember the planning sheet that was in three columns? You just brainstormed a whole bunch of synonyms in each column, because there was no controlled vocabulary on the open Net, and then you'd begin to look at the results. I believe that, in the infancy of the Internet, we were all novice users and we all had to relearn what would and wouldn't work in a new kind of environment.

I love that you think about this in terms of Piaget and developmental skills. Could we talk about what the developmental issues are for K–8 when you're teaching about searching? What do you need to think about, and what can kids do?

Hmmm, the essential skills of searching … What a young student—grades 2, 3, 4, even kindergarten—has to understand is that to look for something is, first, to know what he or she hopes to find. So when a kindergarten kid comes in and wants to find something on the Internet or from the library, what's really important are the questions that the child asks. You'll get a directive like "I need to do a report on cats" or "I need to find a kind of spider." What's very helpful in a situation like that is to ask the student what questions about cats or spiders they want to answer. Respect the question. "If you were to find the very best Web page in the world about cats or spiders, what would it look like?" What kind of result would be the very best response? Ideally, you can do that offline. But most times kids are just going to sit in front of the computer and type, and you have to respect that. You have to respect that that child's first instinct will be to go to that box on the screen, sometimes even go to the URL box, and type in the word "cat."

So, instead of trying to create a rigid formula for how one does this, it's very important to start where the user is. If the kid is going to type the word "cat" in the box, that's what you start with. You don't say to the kid, "Wait a minute, first you've got to get offline and make a list of all the synonyms for cat, the kind of cat you want to find," and so forth. You can't do that; it doesn't respect the child's inquisitiveness.

How do you move a student into thinking just a little bit about improving their searches?

Let the kid do it; let the kid see the results. The only way I'm going to change my behavior is if my results aren't productive. If the results are productive, if the kid gets one good Web site about cats by typing in "cat" in the URL space, there's nothing you can say that's going to make that kid think about changing his behavior. What you have to do is say, "Okay, let's look at this Web page and see if it has *everything* you need. If it doesn't have everything you need, then we can go back and revise our search."

So the important thing is not doing it top-down, but bottom-up, based on a kid's real understanding of what he is doing.

Right. If the child doesn't see a need, then you can't teach it. However, you can help the child see the need; you can go back and say to the student, "What's missing here? What questions do you still have that we haven't been able to answer with this page?" These are evaluation skills. You teach by thinking aloud and by modeling cognitive and metacognitive strategies.

That way you're also respecting a child's integrity. You prefer this approach to, say, a traditional classroom, lecture-type situation?

Oh, definitely. In reality, the reason why a lot of information literacy programs really turn kids off—and I'm talking about through adolescence—is that the librarian comes in with the mindset that he or she knows how to do it right, and that if you'll only just do this, it'll be done and you'll get it right and you'll do a great report. Unfortunately, that removes critical thinking from the process. And that's what we're really teaching. The more important thing, the *most* important thing, that we can teach is critical thinking—clarification, inference, evaluation. Search strategies, search terms, all that stuff is going to get easier and easier. Google [15], Teoma [36], they're all trying to make it easier for the person who doesn't know how to search to get good enough results. That's not a bad thing. You have to start where the person is.

Does that mean that we abandon any idea of teaching this stuff formally?

It depends on which you care about—the means or the end. You can get students to do what you tell them to do. They'll follow if you tell them, "First you put together a search, and then you combine these terms, and then you write the plus sign ...," and so on. But to give that information right off the top is to create the impression of a routine, a formula, as opposed to an algorithm or a recursive thinking process.

And it's not likely to stick. Another problem is that this is a landscape that's in total flux. Those plus signs work or don't work; they're assumed or not assumed. You wind up teaching every single interface, and it's "this didn't work, let me check the 'tips' page and see why it didn't work, let me figure out how to fix it."

You're exactly right. You end up teaching the tool instead of the thinking. Perhaps it's a stereotype that librarians teach information literacy, a thinking process, while technology teachers focus on technology literacy—how to use the tools, period, rather than how to use the tools to acquire learning strategies. I suspect that, in both cases, there are teachers who train students to perform the steps while others focus on the thinking behind those steps.

So do we move on from the messing around, or are we always messing around? Sometimes I feel like we're always messing around.

I believe adults need to mess around, too. School librarians and teachers who operate under a deadline mentality might not be willing to encourage the disequilibrium that's essential to "messing around." But that's a key element in developing a spirit of inquiry.

As a matter of fact, your strategy of asking younger children "what would the very best Web page on your subject look like?" is what I do when I work with adults.

It's common sense. I know you teach that way. The thing is, both you and I, and probably a whole bunch of other really smart people, get sucked in because we hear someone talk about *Google Hacks* [183], for instance, and we say, "Oh, we've got to teach this." But Tara Calishain, the woman who wrote *Google Hacks*, figured all that out by messing around, didn't she?

So that brings up the question, again, of what your ultimate aim is for the learner. In terms of just-in-time learning, you're coaching somebody through a process: "Well, if you know that you really have to have that word appear on the page, you'd better put a plus sign in front of it, because that means that the word must appear." That's such easy learning when you are ready for it. When you need it.

It is. As kids go through K–8 or K–12, what else should they know about? The concept that there is an "AND" out there that might help you, however it's expressed, is good to know about. And you might find it on the initial interface or, if messing around isn't working, you might find it on the advanced search page, or you might find it in the "tips" area. Is there anything else that's important for kids to figure out?

We mentioned one, which is asking yourself "Why aren't my results working?" That's a good question for kids to learn. In reading, a kid asks, "Why am I not understanding what I'm reading?" On the search page, the question is "Why is it that I keep doing this but I'm not getting really good stuff? Even if I'm adding these extra words, it isn't really getting me what I need." So the "why" question, born of a certain frustration level, is another thing kids need to learn. They need to learn that, when the process breaks down, they *can* ask questions.

In reading, they say that what good readers do is learn to recognize when comprehension breaks down. That's exactly what you want to teach kids here. But some reading teachers will tell you that they need to learn that there are five different structures for paragraphs, or they need to learn what boldface text means. Those strategies are the equivalent of teaching the tools. For every rule like that, for every discrete little skill, you're going to find some text that follows the rule, and some text that doesn't. It's much more important for the learner to become a questioner.

You mentioned that they might look at the "tips" or the help page. Yes, for some search engines, looking at the help page is useful. But I find that sometimes the help page is out of date. So even strategies like that are not *always* helpful. With Google, for example, one day a particular feature is working, and the next day they've changed it. Things are changing so quickly. I think kids know that instinctively, whereas adults tend to want to impose structure. Adults, teachers in particular, are trying to assess. To assess, you want that moving target to be still, to "control" the process, or you're going to have to do a whole lot of assessing on the fly.

With all this change going on, how can we guide? Are there any enduring concepts that children can rely on, that they can pack in their mental toolkits?

One important thing for kids to do is to *clump* search tools, that is, to categorize them and understand that certain kinds of search tools are good for certain things. For instance, the

Invisible Web, the huge portion of the Web that's not easily accessible using a general purpose search engine, requires a certain kind of searching. Again, it means envisioning your results: What do I need? If I need a picture from early California, that's American history. Sounds like that's a graphical image. I may have to go to American Memory [83], but I'll never find it by searching on the free Web. You have to develop an understanding that some of the important sites are invisible to search engines like Google.

How do you get kids to learn stuff like that, when they're likely to remember maybe just two or three search engine URLs? Is there a schema that helps kids look at the whole gamut of search tools, helps them build an awareness that there are free databases from which you can get those images?

That's the way you have to start them thinking about using search tools. If they come and look up cats, that's where you start with them. But if they come and say, "I need a photograph of the California Gold Rush, but I typed it into the catalog, or into a Web search engine, and it's not getting me anything," then you can begin to have a conversation around that frustration. You're really building up a set of understandings over time. Your goal is to have them understand that search tools come in clumps.

What kinds of clumps? How does Debbie Abilock view these clumps?

News is one. Shopping is another. You have the Invisible Web clump. Ready reference, because things like dictionaries and encyclopedias—all kinds of reference books—benefit from being online. One Look [31], for instance, is really nice because it doesn't necessarily ask you whether you want to define a word or just get more information. It searches for words and phrases and gathers definitions, translations, and spelling advice based on word patterns from more than 900 online dictionaries. That's real added value.

Are subscription databases another clump?

Yes, but practically speaking, there are only a few databases that most very young students will use: the Kids InfoBits [60] package from Gale, eLibrary [55] from ProQuest, World Book Online [74]. They're not going to use the sophisticated academic databases. For the K–12 market, we can name the five to six or so databases that we feel are really useful for the curriculum. There's a tool called JAKE (Jointly Administered Knowledge Environment) [120] that helps you find journals within electronic databases; it points you to the database that has the journal you need. JAKE is a free tool that any school librarian can use.

But imagine that a kid gets an assignment to go to *Scientific American* and find an article on biology. Sounds like a really easy assignment, doesn't it? It does to a kid and to a teacher, but it doesn't to a librarian. You have to understand what biology is, which of the articles in *Scientific American* fall under that category, where you're going to find *Scientific American*, how to pick an article that's at a reading level you can manage … We can make a list of all the problems with that kind of assignment.

Subscription databases represent quality to us, but you could make a case—and this is probably anathema to the vendors—that what school librarians would really like to be able to do is pick five terrific magazines to subscribe to and be able to search across them electronically using common controlled vocabulary as well as free-text searching. I don't think they'd want us to cherry-pick like that. But in fact some vendors are repackaging material to meet narrower needs. For example, ProQuest offers special regional packages. Schools can subscribe to a database like ProQuest's Newsstand [69] that allows them to select what newspapers, or collections of newspapers, like national newspapers, they'd like their students to use. Gale has discipline-based packages such as the new Science Resource Center [63]. Often you'll get back results that overwhelm. Then you have to have kids evaluate: "Well, do you really want the news from this particular journal? It's not that good." But if we could clump, it would be very helpful.

Scirus [33], the science-specific search tool, sort of does that on its advanced search screen. It allows you to pick out the discipline, to say I want science journals, or I want peer-reviewed journals, I want this or that. It could be even better if it had those five titles that we love.

Debbie, you had one of the first school library Web pages I remember. How would you organize a school Web page now that creates a schema for all these search clumps?

It has to be about curriculum. Just as in our print landscape we can't, and shouldn't, replicate the public library collection, which is a balanced collection for the entire community about all kinds of topics. The school library collection and the school library Web page should reflect three things: the curriculum of the school, the interests and needs of the faculty, and the interests and needs of the students. That allows you leeway to select outside the curriculum, because a kid may have a tremendous passion for racing cars, say, which is nowhere represented in the curriculum, and yet is really important to developing that child as an independent, passionate, inquisitive learner.

In the same way, a Web page needs to be specific. Recently I was a guest speaker in a library school class; a professor was teaching Web page design to school librarians and asked me to come in. That professor has done some fine work on Web page design himself, and school library Web pages. But many of the students were merely replicating his categories and resources. I asked them, "Why don't you just link to his page?" Why bother to replicate it? If somebody else is going to do all the link management for you and create this wonderful site, link to it, and then *you* create the stuff that's different.

That makes perfect sense. But you did some very original work when you were maintaining your page.

And it was all specifically related to our curriculum.

But now you're sharing in a larger world with NoodleTools. What did you hope to accomplish with the site?

NoodleTools actually consists of two or three large areas. The first is NoodleBib, which is *not* a bibliographic citation creator. It is an attempt to teach children—and in fact we find that we're teaching teachers—how to understand how bibliographies are created, the purpose of bibliographies, how to understand what type of source you are looking at.

The wizard in it actually promotes a kind of critical thinking.

Right. It's a teaching tool. If you teach citation correctly, it's really about all the important issues that you want to teach. If you're looking at author, you can teach authority. If you're looking at which online subscription service a document comes from, you can teach credibility. If you're looking at date, you can teach currency. It makes no sense to teach citation as simply a formula: Here's where you put the author's name, then the period. NoodleBib tries to alleviate that by entering the non-thinking parts of a citation automatically. It fills in the punctuation. It creates the correct spacing. That leaves the teacher free to work with students on the important parts of citation, identifying, and discussing the elements.

Initially I thought that this part of your suite of tools didn't have anything to do with searching, but it does. It makes people consider that the end of the process is not necessarily the end; it sends them back in the recursive way that we want kids to think about information use in its larger sense.

That's right. The better NoodleBib is at conveying that, the more teachers will understand and use it as that kind of tool. For example, it seems to me that teachers talk a lot about how kids will not use a source because they don't know how to cite it. But they also talk about kids including sources that don't have anything to do with what they are investigating. Well, if you require kids to annotate their source lists, you are asking them to identify the key elements of why they've chosen it.

Annotating is reflective; it's metacognitive. It focuses on the process. We discovered that, when a student does all this legwork—the evaluation, the selection, and the reflection—the formal written project may not really have to be completed at all.

So you could literally just create the authorities.

Right. The authority's there, and then the student demonstrates the knowledge in some way—by chatting, performing ...

I think the reflective piece is really important. So that's one clump of NoodleTools.

I like the concept of clumping because it is a metaphor for a lot of what we do with kids and a lot of the things we need to teach.

You don't teach a tool, you teach types, clumps of tools. You don't teach a search engine, you teach types of search engines. Another clump on NoodleTools is my experimental thinking around teaching reading. I believe that the first step in understanding how to learn within a discipline is understanding that that discipline has a language. In math that's obvious; it's a set of numbers and letters. That's the basic toolkit. But it's also about how math creates a sentence or an idea or a problem, how math speaks. It's the same thing with science and with humanities. Each of those disciplines has a language; there's a code that you need to decode in order to learn to read fluently.

Those attack skills, the strategies for decoding and making sense of text while reading, come into play as kids look at result lists or go through the stuff they've printed out.

I believe that online reading is an important part of what we need to be teaching. There is a group of people at AASL who believe that school librarians should not be teaching reading. I think that reading is an access issue. Some might define "access" as locating stuff. But access is also finding what you need *within* the information that you locate. And teaching reading—online reading, print reading, visual reading—for the purpose of access is exactly what we need to be doing. Web reading is a whole lot different from print reading.

What is effective Web reading for you? What does it look like?

Some research has been done. It says that kids look at the words on a Web page before they look at images. But I'm not sure that will continue. It may be that, the more visually attuned kids become, the more they will "read" visual images first. Apparently our kids still get meaning from text, probably headline text, before they get meaning from an image. It may be that image reading is still hard for them, especially since we're not teaching much of it in school. But we have to learn what kids are doing, and then we have to show them how to improve whatever "reading" they're doing in that context.

It isn't a simple thing. You don't say to kids, "When you're reading a Web page, this is what you do first and this is what you do second." But as you see what kids *are* doing, again, it's not top-down, it's bottom-up. It's constructing. You'll say to a kid, "The stuff in bold across the top there, in that box, is an ad." Kids often think the ads are part of the results they've gotten. Teachers who are teaching kids how to construct Web pages need to teach from Web pages that exist. A kid is not going to construct a Web page with an ad, so understanding what an ad is will be off the kid's radar. If you're going to teach a kid about navigating using "bread crumbs," the best way to do that is to show them why they need bread crumbs to make it easier to navigate their Web site. Bread crumbs show the user where he or she is on every page of the site; they visually display the hierarchical trail from the top or "home" level to the next level to the current page.

A lot of people rave about "Choose the Best Search for Your Information Need" [92] on NoodleTools. It's your clumping again.

> Yes, it's my clumping. It takes a hell of a long time to do and redo. It's not just a question of keeping the links fresh. When I sit down to do a revision, I start with fresh thinking about what I am missing, what's out of my radar, what's coming up that I'm not looking at. This time I focused on some of the search engines that sort results into categories, the way Northern Light [30] did.

Laura Cohen [94] in Albany talks about that as horizontal searching. It allows us to see results in clusters we may never have seen going page by page by page down a traditional result list. It helps with evaluation, similar to the way NoodleTools forces kids to evaluate as they develop documentation. Are there other ways we can work with kids on evaluation and critical thinking, on separating the drek from the better stuff?

> When kids read a piece of garbage—name any book that you think is poorly written—how do they recognize it's garbage until they've read a really fine book? It's only in contrast to good stuff that kids recognize garbage. It's only in contrast to a good Martin Luther King site, a Martin Luther King site that explains what this man's legacy is in some balanced context, that kids will recognize, "My goodness, *this* is a hate site!" It's interesting to me that people talk about print authority versus Web authority. The Ku Klux Klan has published books. So authority is not some black-and-white criterion about being "in print." Encyclopedias have been produced for the K–12 market that have unauthoritative science information. Particular entries are inaccurate. They're in print. They've been vetted. They've gone through a process. But knowledge changes. Editors are imperfect. I hope we help kids understand what I didn't understand when I was a kid. I remember reading an entry in one encyclopedia long ago; fairly recently I had an opportunity to look at that edition again and to realize

how racist it was. I didn't recognize the racism then, swimming in the water of my culture at that period in history, with the education I had had to that point.

Let's shift gears a bit. What trends are you seeing? What's the Web going to look like for kids a few years down the road?

There's a lot of consolidation going on in terms of search engines. Very simple, broad-based searches are going to get better and better for kids. Clustering and visual interface tools like Mooter [27], Visual Thesaurus [38], and Vivisimo [39] may help students brainstorm synonyms and related terms for a search. The idea of the Invisible Web—which shouldn't be invisible but is—will change as federated searching gets better. For now, federated searching is a blunt tool. Federated searching is the effort to take a variety of different databases, search them individually based on the patron's need, and create a set of helpful results. Federated searching creates a search query for each separate database—an intensive programming job at present, without controlled vocabulary or common agreements about fields from database to database.

When you add a federated search to your library catalog, you work with the software people to decide how the results should appear. Some librarians want the results from the library's catalog to appear before the free Web results, for example. Federated search packages like Muse [131] or WebFeat [41] are configured to search each of the fee-based databases that the library owns and provide results in clumped categories ordered by currency. This has tremendous benefits, because it integrates your Gale resources and your ProQuest resources with the free Web and with the library catalog. Is it a good tool right now? No. It's a blunt tool right now. It's not good enough. And the reason that it's not good enough is that you search Gale one way, you search your library catalog another way, and Gale's output is different from your library catalog's output. It's a challenge to make that all transparent to the user. It will make it easier for the novice user.

But you risk losing a sense of where the information comes from. You may not be able to figure out whether you're looking at an e-book version of a print book, at something from Gale's humanities database, or at something from the free Web that Mikey Junior put up for his class. The context of information is important and you risk losing it when results are integrated.

Word relevance is a context problem, as well. For instance, if you're searching literary criticism in Gale's Literature Resource Center [61], "criticism" is not necessarily a meaningful term. However, you need to include it when you're searching your library catalog and general databases; you want Steinbeck and you also want literary criticism. The searching context varies so much.

Yes, federated searching doesn't obviate the need for the learner to understand what the context is. For example, when you teach the literary criticism database, you teach that it has "authority" by virtue of peer review and vetting. How do you teach that when the results come in unattached to a source? You have to teach it in terms of "let's look at the result, let's look at where it comes from, who wrote it, and does it fit with what you know already?" It's almost backward.

Right. And so much of this seems to happen as over-the-shoulder teaching, the informal learning that goes on as you work with individual, just-in-time questions around the lab or library. I've also moved to pathfinders as a kind of independent teaching strategy. You don't want to lecture or preach; but I worry that, if we don't grab them now ...

The first year that I worked in a school, I was told what to teach. It was a part-time job and I was coming into a situation where the head of the school had decided that she would teach research because she had been an academic researcher. All I was going to teach was the supplemental stuff. I spent the entire year trying to teach kids the difference between looking something up through the alphabetical letters of *World Book* and looking in the index. My problem was that there was no need for them to know this. The key to really teaching searching or information literacy is to design curriculum. It's not until our students care desperately to find the right information that you will get them to learn what you want them to know.

Super Searcher Power Tips

➤ Ask the learner to explain what he or she needs and how it will be used. As the learner explains, starting with what is likely an unformed and as yet inexplicit thought, it becomes clearer to both of you which sources, search terms, and strategies could be useful.

➤ Think aloud as you construct a search with your students and teachers. You are modeling, *exactly at the moment when the learner is open to understanding*, the relevant cognitive strategies he or she might use in a future search.

➤ Learn to recognize and anticipate the common progression of feelings, thoughts, and actions that learners of any age experience during an information search. A Super Searcher teacher develops skill in diagnosing the searcher's problems, determining the most effective interventions and providing ongoing feedback to improve search performance.

➤ Read about search developments voraciously, but in a practical way that won't overwhelm you. For example, I'm using Yahoo!'s News Beta RSS [48] feed to keep up with search engine changes. Another way to learn search engine strategies is to monitor changes on the "Choose the Best Search for Your Information Need" Web page using Change Detect.

➤ Learn Google well, since that's what your novices are familiar with, by using the syntax commands or the advanced page.

➤ Practice customizing your own results to fit your own needs. For example, for a book I'm writing, I have Watch That Page [163] monitoring several important Web pages and a search running in Bloglines [6] on the term "plagiarism."

➤ Teach by comparing. Open two browser windows and use them in tandem. While Vivisimo's clustering helps you find buried results, Teoma helps you find authoritative sites. Which is more useful for this particular search task? When might the other be a first choice?

➤ Teach your students to think about who is likely to collect and organize the information you're searching for. For example, when I am beginning to research a topic, I use Amazon's A9 [1] search (which returns results from Google and from Amazon's "Search Inside the Book") in order to identify relevant books.

➤ Teach your teachers to search. Your students will learn for life in a schoolwide community of searchers who are trading tips and strategies, rather than just taking lessons from one lone Super Searcher.

Marjorie Pappas
The Role of Process

Marjorie Pappas has been a middle school librarian, an administrator of school libraries, and a library science professor at Wright State University in Ohio, the University of Northern Iowa, and Eastern Kentucky University. Co-author of the *Pathways to Knowledge* [193, see Appendix] model for information literacy, she regularly publishes articles and books on information literacy and electronic searching. Pappas is an active member of AASL [75] and is currently associate professor and chair of the online distance School Library and Information Technologies master's program at Mansfield University of Pennsylvania.

mpappas@mansfield.edu
http://library.mnsfld.edu

**Marjorie, you created the *Pathways to Knowledge* model.
Can you talk to me about the role of process in student searching?**

I am an absolute believer in teaching kids a process for searching. It's like a recipe. As a middle school librarian, I taught them about specific resources. I taught them about the dictionary, the encyclopedia, the *Reader's Guide* [70], and the card catalog. I taught them to use specific resources and tools, but this instruction was typically out of context; I did not teach so that students could make the lesson applicable each time they had another searching task. I found that when the task changed, they were back at my elbow, because the previous lessons were either forgotten or did not apply. They could not extrapolate from one task to the next one. So those experiences led to collaboration with Ann Tepe and the creation of an information process model, *Pathways to Knowledge*. At about the same time, school library professionals were also developing process models. Carol Kuhlthau had completed her research and developed the Information Search Process [207]. Michael Eisenberg and Robert Berkowitz developed the Big6 [184]. Barbara Stripling and Judy Pitts created a similar information process within their book *Brainstorms and Blueprints* [201]. Jamie McKenzie's *The Research Cycle* [104] was published about that same time. The concept of information seeking as a process has slowly evolved over time.

Do these various models share some common elements?

Absolutely. In fact, Ann and I wrote a paper on that topic for one of the Treasure Mountain Research Retreats [192]. I was looking for commonalities, so, out of that ministudy, I created a comparison chart that listed the major concepts or steps in the left column, and examined where those major steps appear across the models, and in some cases the steps that were missing. It gave a person looking at models a quick way to find which concepts or steps appear in each one.

In my information literacy courses, I've asked students to examine and use models. I think individuals have to eventually pick a model that feels right and internalize it, perhaps tweak it a bit, so it works for the individual, because our learning styles are all different. I have even asked students to create their own model. That has been a project in some of my courses.

For your graduate students?

Yes. Create your own model, and do it with graphics, so that it's more of a tutorial, not just a list of textual steps. The goal is to visually depict how the model would flow. Name it something that has meaning. Some of my students now have these models on their Web sites; they're very proud of them.

Do you think people need to visualize the search process?

Yes, I do. If you visit the Big6 Web site [88], for example, you'll see more and more organizers to help students visualize an information-seeking process. It becomes a road map or a pathfinder.

I did notice that your *Pathways to Knowledge* model had concentric circles suggesting an iterative process.

Ann Tepe and I felt that was very important to convey. We both believe that the information seeking process is nonlinear.

You illustrate that with arrows going back and forth across the circles.

Anytime you put it on paper you're working with a flat linear surface. But we did everything we could to give the appearance of recursion, going back and forth among the stages. There are places in the process where you work your way so far, and then something happens that causes you to have to return to a previous stage.

And you say uh-oh, I missed something, or I need to go back and look at something again.

Exactly, or changes occur. There are so many different variables that can make a searcher have to back up. Think about the way we teach kids to write; that's a similar process. Teachers have tried to teach students that this process also is recursive. The notion that you sit down, create, write a paper, and you're done is ludicrous.

Right, there's no such thing as a final draft.

Teaching that notion, not only to students in the writing process but also in the process of searching, gathering, and using information, is really important. So often they want to just find information and finish the project—"Whatever I've gathered, I'm done. This is it, I'm writing on what I've gathered"—rather than evaluating the information they've gathered, looking for omissions, looking for the need in some places to embellish what was missed in the original search. They just want to get it done, so they don't back up. I think it's really important for students to understand the recursive nature of the process, that it has a nonlinear feel to it.

In order to accomplish that with students, we have to get teachers on board, in the same way that they have adopted the writing process. We need them as partners, and we need them to realize that some student deadlines—like come up with a thesis for tonight's homework—just might not work.

Exactly. There has to be some flexibility. On the other hand, you can't say to students, "Well, it's due whenever you get it done." We're all human; we'll all put it off. So there has to be some structure. I think graphic organizers provide excellent structure. Inside those organizers, teachers and students can work together to determine a reasonable deadline—knowing that, within the framework of that reasonable deadline, there has to be some willingness to say, in conversation with an individual student, "I can see where you need to back up, let's give you a couple more days to gather additional information and revise the product."

Marjorie, can we get a little more tangible at this point? We've been talking about these models and their common elements, and I'd like to talk a little bit more about what they look like.

Pathways, the model I know intimately, starts with Appreciation, which is unique. That stage appears in very few of the models. Appreciation provides a beginning stage for discovery where that is appropriate. But not every information seeker begins with that stage. When you look at this process, you may decide you want to start at the Searching stage. Maybe in a previous paper or activity you've already done what I would consider to be the Presearch stage of this model, and you want to get engaged right at the Search stage. In this model you start wherever your needs are.

If you want to look at the holistic approach, the Appreciation stage focuses on developing student curiosity, engaging then in discovery. Presearch is the stage that focuses on making connections to prior knowledge. That's really important from a constructivist point of view. We need to encourage teachers to help learners make a connection with prior knowledge. That is one of the first steps librarians do; we always work at making that connection. What's the first thing we do if we don't know anything about a topic, when we have no concept and can't put it into a discipline? We go to an encyclopedia or a dictionary, trying to find related disciplines. That's making the connection to prior knowledge.

Can you suggest strategies for motivating students to make those connections?

Okay, to take this to the realm of the practical, I have a good friend in Ohio, a former student, Gayle Geitgey. Gayle is now a high school librarian and district school technology coordinator. She created a hall pass that requires students to consider these connections *on their way to* the library. It's a half sheet of paper. In order to come to the library, the student must have that piece of paper in his or her hand. On the pass is a simple web diagram that asks students to do some initial brainstorming, leading them to answer the question "What do I already know about my topic?" before they arrive at the library. On the back side of the pass is another little organizer that asks, "What are some resources I could use to begin my search; where might I begin to find general information about my topic?"

If they come to the library and they haven't completed the form, Gayle sits them down and says, "Okay, let's look at this together. What is it that you're looking for? What do you already know? Let's go into brainstorming mode." She is teaching them to think that way before they begin a search. It helps students generate keywords. When they plunge right in with whatever words hit the top of their heads, their searches are often not very successful. But if they work with a simple organizer and try to think about related topics, they will have a better sense of what their topic is related to. It helps them ultimately be more effective searchers.

And, as a bonus, students recognize the value of the librarian acting as an adult mentor in the pre-search process.

Yes. Speaking of mentoring, if I can digress a bit, your work with pathfinders has always intrigued me. So I've built pathfinders into the courses I'm teaching. When I taught reference the last several semesters, my students had to create a pathfinder. This was a new concept for many of them. There are different kinds of pathfinders. Many are just a list of references available on the Web. I am far more interested in the absolute definition of the pathfinder, which is literally a pathway for gathering and using information. So I asked students to identify an information model of their choice that would underpin the pathfinder. I encourage them to join two concepts together—the information process model and the pathfinder. The design of the pathfinder must follow the steps or stages of the information process model.

So a pathfinder might address your Appreciation stage with a suggestion of something to view or understand, to understand why this area that we're studying is exciting and important. Then the Presearch stage might suggest some keywords, or where you might begin to look for keywords or phrases.

Yes, and it might also include some general resources to help students find initial background information. It might include a brainstorming organizer, where they could start to develop some questions. They would use organizers to generate some initial keywords related to their topic. It should also offer a space, before they ever get to the search step, that literally asks, "What is my research question?" Without that initial research question to define their search, when they reach the point where they are trying to evaluate the information they have gathered, they are evaluating against air.

The people who contribute to the Big6 Web site are doing exactly the same thing. When they get into the search part of the process, or perhaps the Presearch, they say, "Here are some sources you might check that will help you build background knowledge. Here are some call numbers that might help you browse. Here are some keywords that might help you search in the catalog or a database. Here are some really, really good reference resources just to get you started. Here's how you might find magazine articles." It's about trying to help students see that there's more to researching than just going to Google [15].

Do you encounter any resistance? When you first introduce the concept of pathfinders, how do your graduate students respond?

A lot of cognitive dissonance goes on when I introduce that pathfinder project. I've had to tell some people, when I assess the pathfinder, "You have to start over. This doesn't work, and this is why." However, many students have created excellent pathfinders, complete with illustrations.

Another section that is important on the pathfinder relates to organizing and evaluating information. Too often students want to go straight from searching to putting it on paper. I believe pathfinders should point students to the tools they need for analysis, evaluation, and synthesis. David Loertscher's article, "All That Glitters May Not Be Gold" [208] addresses what I would call the Interpretation stage of the process, that is, the organization and evaluation of information before the writing begins. We need to give students more visual organizers. Does the task require a comparison? If so, what organizer can I use to compare? Does the task require synthesis? What organizer can I use to synthesize? There are so many Web sites available that contain excellent organizer collections. Graphic Organizers.org [108] has a list of organizers.

Or the librarian might introduce some generic tools that the kids can recreate using Inspiration [117] or Word. Or students could brainstorm ideas in bubbles with pencil and paper. Being able to create these mental tools is powerful. I love to watch or help students create them as I conference with them. You can see them thinking.

I think there is a developmental progression here. If I were working with primary children, I would hand them an organizer designed for the task. "Worksheet" is a four-letter word in my vocabulary; it just doesn't allow for much creativity and independent thought. In the beginning, we need to do more modeling and slowly give students the power to create and select their own organizers. At intermediate levels we offer a selection. "Here are three you might use. You pick the one that works the best for you." By high school, an assessment of whether they really understand this concept is whether they can design their own organizer to fit a specific task. Organizers are especially helpful in the part of the process that is often the most difficult for student searchers: How do I organize my information? How do I bridge the gap between all the information that's out there and the product I ultimately need to create?

And how do I maintain my voice as a writer as I'm doing it.

Yes, and that's really important. I had completed my doctoral program before I understood that I had the right to a voice. During that era, there was a stylized, very formulaic kind of writing; basically, you didn't have an opinion. You could rephrase, but you had to base everything on what others wrote. But we can develop scaffolds to help students make bridges. They can go from the voices of others to, "Okay, now let's put that all away. What do *I* know as a result of what I've read, and what patterns do *I* see?"

I see organizing as critical in all the processes—in collecting information, in structuring the product. You keep looking for those patterns and figuring out how the

information you select and your original thoughts fit together. What do you think is important for learners to consider when they are actively *searching*?

In the *Pathways* model, Ann and I identified four different kinds of search strategies: Explore, Browse, Hierarchical, and Analytical. In the Explore mode, I am just hopping from one Web site to another. I have no plan; it's sort of serendipitous, a discovery of new information.

That happens in the early stages as we begin to figure out what we're looking at.

And teachers can develop an organizer even for that. It may seem scattered, but we have to let some of that happen. That's related to brainstorming and Presearching. Browsing is related to a linear index like a catalog or a print index. When I'm using an index in a printed book, that's browsing.

When you're looking through a Dewey number, you're browsing the shelves in the same way.

Yes, although some of that is more related to what we would define as Explore. A Hierarchical search starts with a short list of broad topics or disciplines. The searcher makes a selection based on her topic and a new, more focused list of topics appears. This process continues until it results in a list of resources.

Many people believe the skills for using a subject directory are the same as the skills for using a search engine, but I don't agree. I believe that it's a totally different kind of searching. You have to know how to follow a hierarchical relationship of information to be effective at using a subject directory. You also have to know something about the topic. A searcher needs to know when a Hierarchical search is appropriate. One of the positives of a Hierarchical search is that the searcher is not required to develop a list of appropriate keywords. That makes a Hierarchical search in a subject directory more appealing to younger or less experienced searchers. On the other hand, an Analytical search requires a searcher to use a relational database like a search engine or a subscription database. For example, searching in Excite [10], AltaVista [3], or EBSCO's Magazine Article Summaries [54] would be an Analytical search. In an Analytical search, the searcher needs a well-developed list of keywords in order to avoid a huge hit list.

Where does selecting among all the potential search tools fit into the process?

Moving on within the model, we address selecting information resources and tools. Instead of pulling a cart of books, we should be asking kids, "What resources would work for this search task of yours?" That's a worthwhile conversation to have with students. If you do that often enough, you put it back on the student; you encourage them to be less dependent on you, the librarian. During this selection process you can say to them, "Evaluate what you've used for other projects when you needed to gather information." From among those resources, ask them "What would be the most useful resource for this new searching task?"

One of my favorite stories is the graduate student a few years back who sat down in front of Compton's electronic encyclopedia on CD-ROM. She was obviously frustrated. She jumped up and was about to leave. I walked over and asked, "What's wrong?" And she said, "Well, they tell us that these electronic things are so wonderful, but what I'm looking for isn't in there." I asked what she was looking for. She replied, "I'm looking for information on the Kentucky Educational Reform Act." I looked at her and asked, "In Compton's?" Of course, I said more to soften that response, but it's a great illustration of the phenomenon that, just because it's electronic, people assume that all of knowledge is contained within it. They don't think about the particular resource in relation to their searching need. We need to teach students this skill. Do I need a periodical index, a search engine, a database? Should I start with books, or should I start with the catalog? Where do I have to start? What tool, and then what resource, would best help me with my search?

I wonder how we expect people to develop an awareness of the tools they have in their toolkit. If this generation of searchers leaves us without that awareness, they'll expect that Google's going to do everything. They won't know, for instance, that ProQuest Historical Newspapers [68] is where you're going to find a contemporaneous newspaper report of the Triangle Shirtwaist fire. You're not likely to find that in Google.

Even with graduate students, I had to say at the beginning of some of our reference activities, "You cannot use Google. You must use other resources to find the answers to these questions, because it is critical that you learn about those resources." You can't rely on Google to put the best references at the very top of the list. Popularity is not the best arbiter of quality. Think of all the information that is available from the Government Printing Office [107] alone. I required students to search some of those resources, because I wanted them to understand that in some cases they will find more appropriate information in those resources.

I'm worried that we're not going to catch this generation of searchers before they become adult searchers. I want my students to know about the tools in their toolkits—when to use the hammer, when to use the wrench. Yet, in the world outside my library, I don't see broader expectations for students to develop this knowledge.

I agree with you 100 percent. It blows me out of the water but I'm not willing to give up, Joyce. Wouldn't it be great if library school courses were offered in universities as a series that any-one could take? We need professional development for librarians *and* for teachers. We need professional development courses that school librarians can take easily—maybe not full-blown courses; maybe six-week workshops. We need some of that material online. I have had conversations with school librarians on several e-mail lists who learned to catalog before there were such things as automated catalogs and MARC records. They need help. They don't need another degree; they just need updated knowledge and skills.

So much to worry about, Marjorie! But let's continue to talk about the process. We discussed selecting tools. What haven't we covered?

As for the Communication stage in the *Pathways* model, searchers often have some concept, all the way through the information-seeking process, of how they're going to use the information. But it's important to help students understand that, once they've gathered the information, pulled it together in a way that it's organized and synthesized and they know what they want to say, then it makes sense to think about the best way to present it. Often, teachers tend to say, "You're going to use this medium to communicate your information," meaning you're going to write a paper or do a PowerPoint or a newsletter or whatever. But as students evolve with the process, we need to give them the latitude of deciding the best medium to use.

Finally, in most models, there is an Evaluation step. It's critical to evaluate the process as well as the product. Every time students complete a project in which they apply an information-seeking process, the teacher or librarian should talk with them—as a group, not necessarily with each individual student—and get them to evaluate their process. What worked? What didn't work? Why didn't it work? What would you do differently next time? That evaluation ought to happen time after time. That's how students learn to internalize a process. One of the things we've learned about problem solving is that the "debriefing" piece is often missing. If we want the new skills to transfer, students need to reflect on the process. They need to talk about what worked and what didn't work.

I like the idea of reflection as a group effort, because there are things people will learn that they wouldn't have learned if it were just a self-reflection.

I agree wholeheartedly. But another good technique is to ask students to take five minutes, brainstorm, and then write a little reflective piece, individually. What do you think was the most successful part of your search? What are some things you would change about your information-seeking process? And then share that knowledge with the group. It's more meaningful when students are not shooting from the hip.

In your experience, does the type of learning that happens during this process become habit after a while?

I think it does, although we don't have enough research to support that hypothesis. There has to be much more research on information-seeking using a process model. We need to build on the body of knowledge we already have.

Back to my worrying, I worry about transference of these skills. Students will do this or that because you tell them to do it, but will they do it when you're not looking? I hope they will.

I think it would be useful to examine, for example, some of the results that came out of the research that Ross Todd did in Ohio recently [211] with successful schools. Ultimately we want to know what happens across the board in all schools with all students. But at this point we have so few schools where this kind of process model instruction is really pursued effectively. We need to start with the schools that are doing it successfully. We need to research whether or not that learning transfers. Do students apply these skills on their own when they have a problem? Or is it only applied with teacher or librarian direction? I think we need a longitudinal research study that investigates what happens after our students graduate and go on to their jobs or function as adults in their families and communities. Do they apply an information process there? We need to look at schools where they use a model all the way through all levels. What happens over time when students go to junior high, and what happens when they go to high school, and then what happens when they leave us? Is the process so internalized that they continue to apply it as a lifelong learning skill, or do they drop it?

It's almost frightening. You won't want to find out if it stops.

Well, if it stops, then the question is why. And we really need to know the answer to that question if we're going to make this thinking process work.

Super Searcher Power Tips

➤ There are many information process models in use today. Librarians, teachers, and individual information seekers are strongly encouraged to select the one that best fits their learning style. The steps below are a generic representation of the various process models. To one degree or another, these steps appear in all models.

➤ Discovery

➤ What topics or ideas pique my curiosity?

➤ What do I already know about my topic?

➤ Develop questions

➤ What is the focus of my search?

➤ What question(s) frame my search?

➤ Locate information

➤ Which tools and resources will help me find information about my topic?

➤ What keywords can I use?

➤ How can I pursue and refine my search strategies to find relevant information?

➤ Evaluate, Organize, and Synthesize

➤ Which organizers will help me sift through all my new information?

➤ What strategies should I use to evaluate my information for accuracy, bias, and relevancy?

➤ Communicate new knowledge

➤ What medium is the most appropriate to communicate my new knowledge?

➤ What tools can I use to develop my product?

➤ Evaluate process and product

➤ How do I evaluate my product?

➤ How do I use reflection to assess my information-seeking process so I will be more effective in my next searching task?

David Barr

Knowledge, Skills, and Attitudes for Successful Searching

David Barr recently retired as Director of Online Learning at the Illinois Mathematics and Science Academy (IMSA), where he directed IMSA's 21st Century Information Fluency Project. David was a member of the writing teams for the Illinois Learning Standards for both students and teachers, and is a member of the Leadership Team for ISTE's (International Society for Technology in Education) National Educational Technology Standards (NETS) project [134, see Appendix].

barr@imsa.edu
http://21cif.imsa.edu

You are not a librarian, David, but I know you as a fellow geek. Tell me about your alternate background in searching.

I came to both searching and technology from the perspective of a teacher, from learning how to use technology to be a better teacher, and with the goal of using technology to help others become better learners.

A lot of techie-interested teachers who move into the kinds of organizations you've been involved with might gravitate toward the hardware side. But you decided to look at interactions between learners and interfaces. How did you develop that specialty?

When I first became interested in using technology in education, you had to know more about hardware and software, and then networks, than you do now. There just weren't that many people around in schools to help you in those areas. So I got involved in installing hardware, administering server systems, and installing networks. But once those were in place, it became clear that the human/technology interface was going to be the most significant obstacle to making good use of technology in education. I've always felt that to help others learn you have to get as close to the process of learning as you can. Watching people use computers in learning environments is a great way to do that.

At IMSA, what projects are you proudest of?

Most of the projects I've been involved in during the past 15 years have been focused on helping people use technology to teach and learn more effectively. But the work we've done to help educators and students learn to locate, evaluate, and use online resources, as part of IMSA's 21st Century Information Fluency Project, has been the most rewarding. That project began with observing teachers and students use computers. Ten years ago, when Illinois schools were just getting the first round of technology funding, new hardware, new software, new networks were being installed in schools, and the Internet was just beginning to become widely available. In my role as IMSA's Director of Statewide Technology Initiatives, I encountered lots of interested teachers who genuinely wanted to help students use these new technologies to learn. But they often felt overwhelmed by all there was to learn about hardware, software, and the Internet all at once. I wanted to help both teachers and students use these tools to help improve student learning.

I gradually realized that if you talked to most of them about techie stuff—hardware, software, even the Internet—their eyes glazed over. But if I asked them what kind of information would help them teach and help their students learn, their eyes lit up. For me, focusing on information turned out to be a much better way to engage people in conversations about teaching and learning than getting involved in platform wars. That's how the project began. Since then it has grown steadily. We've now worked with more than 200 schools. We're funded to work directly with Illinois schools, but as you know many of our learning materials and software tools are available to everyone through our portal [113]. I also take every opportunity to thank our funders: The IMSA Fund for the Advancement of Education [114], IBM [110], Ameritech, now SBC [146], the Polk Brothers Foundation [143], the Lumpkin Foundation [127], and the U.S. Department of Education Fund for the Improvement of Education [161].

So what works? What have you learned relating to these 21st-century literacies or fluencies? How have you helped?

Where to begin? First, I'll say that we've learned that these 21st-century literacies or fluencies—we use literacy to refer to the basics and fluency to describe more complex abilities—are not just skill sets. They involve knowledge, skills, and attitudes. What we've discovered in this area is shown visually in a model we've developed [116]. The model describes the knowledge, skills, and attitudes relating to the resources, strategies, and tools needed to locate, evaluate, and use digital information resources. The cube illustrates 27 categories that help us focus on what's important as we develop learning materials, tools, and experiences.

So it's a schema or a way for people to understand the components of digital information literacy.

Yes, the 27 blocks in that cube describe most of the things we think people need in order to become more efficient and effective as searchers. For example, knowledge about the strategies needed to evaluate digital information resources, or skills in using tools to locate digital information resources, or attitudes about materials that we are going to use as evidence in a presentation. Though some are more important than others, the model clarifies the interrelationship of those different literacies and fluencies. In other words, when we watch people succeed, we see that they use a combination of knowledge, skills, and attitudes. Like most complex human abilities, using information is a systems problem. The total is more than the sum of the parts. You have to acquire particular knowledge, skills, and attitudes, *and* you have to be able to use them together. This model describes a cluster of knowledge, skills, and attitudes that we believe are needed for effective searching. They have to be used together, but they aren't typically taught or learned together.

Of course, you have to start with where people are, and provide them an inviting entry point, a place to start. For younger students and beginning learners we developed our "Top Ten Tips," [115] some years ago, because those were the 10 things we saw as the top time-wasters.

What would be an example of a top-ten time-waster?

When we developed them, the number-one time-waster I observed was looking for things on the Internet that weren't there. So, Top Ten Tip number one was: "If it isn't there, don't look for it." That may seem obvious, but if students make the wrong strategic decision about where to search, teaching them tactics about how to search doesn't help. We saw a lot of people, especially when the Internet was smaller, wasting a lot of time looking in the wrong place. Unfortunately, that's still true today. The tips are practical, aphoristic statements of the knowledge, skills, and attitudes required that we developed from watching successful and unsuccessful searches.

What are some of the things you discovered as you watched students search well or poorly? What weren't they able to do easily, and how do the tools you are developing help?

There are many good models of the search process. For the sake of simplicity, we break it down into a few simple questions. The first question is *what*: What am I looking for? The next question is *where*: Where should I look for it? The third is *how*: What tools, techniques, and tips could I use to get there? The last is *what next*: Am I done? If not, what's the next step?

A successful search usually involves going through this cycle repeatedly until you're done. As someone once said, searching is a process, not an event. We suggest that students ask themselves these questions repeatedly, and we try to provide interfaces that make this easier for them. This may seem obvious to many, but it isn't intuitive for many students.

What you're describing is a kind of wizard that provokes the thoughts that you would expect kids to come up with on their own after they've had some better search experiences.

Yes. For each of those questions, a lot of people make default decisions, without even knowing it. The typical student who is given a question and goes to the Web has answered the question "where" in a very simplistic manner. The same for the "how" question. They usually have two or three favorite things to try, and when those don't work, they don't have anything to fall back on. Part of the task of helping people learn to search is giving them a larger bag of tricks, a larger number of options in each one of those question areas.

So you've identified some very specific skills that wizard-type questioning might help learners develop. Can you give me some examples of those questions? What do the wizards actually do?

For example, in the "what" category of the process, students often don't know how to move from question to query. Their question is usually a natural language statement. A question might be something like, "How many buffalo are there left in the wild in America today?" That's a question stated in natural language growing directly out of the discipline and the research that's being done. That question has to be turned into a query that consists of keywords. The first step might be getting rid of stop words that won't help with the search. The second is based on understanding that a single concept can be described using many different words.

How do you demonstrate to learners what a solid query would look like?

Let's consider that query about how many buffalo are left. Eventually you have to look for synonyms for buffalo, because if you enter "buffalo" you get the city of Buffalo, the Buffalo Bills, and similar things. Eventually you discover that a good synonym for *buffalo* is *bison*. If you're looking for a good synonym for *number of* it turns out to be *population*. Those are the terms that people who write in this field are most likely to use. Understanding that the people who create Web pages don't always use the same terms you would is a fundamental concept.

Do you find learners impatient about getting to that point? The student would have to do significant reading, or at least some serious gleaning from results, to get from that question to that query, right?

You ask about impatience. As I said earlier, we're interested in knowledge, skills, and attitudes. Among the most important of the attitudes we find in successful searchers are patience and persistence. We have to help learners acquire the *attitudes* needed for successful searching as well as the knowledge and skills required. We can help them do that in several ways. For example, we can provide timesaving tools such as a thesaurus, and more intuitive interfaces, and one-stop shopping in the form of a kind of Web metasearch facility. All these can help students feel they are being more efficient, and save them time. Once they see that persistence can pay off, they are more likely to begin developing patience.

Of course, a thesaurus is just a tool, not a strategy. We encourage students to use a "triangulation" strategy. You might first look at a thesaurus, and then scan the summaries in a search engine's results list, and then look at some promising documents. If you look at those three things and compare them, or triangulate, you'll typically find that one or two terms surface as the most used and the most likely to be useful to you.

But students must go beyond interacting with the search box to do some independent thinking. How do we encourage them to develop this patience, this curiosity, this interest in accessing really good stuff? In fact, how do we move them toward the knowledge that there's good stuff and maybe not-so-good stuff out there?

We certainly don't have answers, but we're conducting some experiments to see what might work or not work. We're testing a software tool we call a practice database, a set of practice searches in which you're given a question very like the one I described, and in which you are then allowed or encouraged to search for relevant and reliable documents. Then you're given feedback on how well you've done at finding the best and most accurate of those documents. So students can begin to get a sense of how well they do.

One of the most difficult things people report about searching the Internet is that they have no idea whether they've gotten good stuff or not, so they tend to just take whatever they get and think that's the best there is. It's the problem of recall. In the information science world, recall has a very precise technical definition; it's the ratio of the number of relevant records retrieved to the total number of relevant records. I'm using the term more loosely to refer to the goal of finding more than one or two relevant documents and, in particular, to finding the most relevant documents. Search engines tend to be focused on getting relevant documents to the top of the list. Search engine users tend to believe that the first hits they get from search engines are the most relevant. And because search engine users seldom read beyond the first page, they also tend to believe that there are not more relevant or useful documents further down the results list, or that a refined search will find even more relevant documents.

Among other things, the practice database is designed to help alert people to the need to dig down further, to refine their searches, and hopefully even to motivate them to find the best documents, not just the first relevant document they find. Many students are overconfident. They think they are getting good results. When we can show them they aren't always getting the best results, or even good enough, it can be motivating.

The problem of recall is particularly important when students are doing genuine research. Questions with one right answer—a fact—can often be answered by one document. What students want is to get that document at the top of the hit list. Search engines tend to be optimized to do that. But when we ask students to explore questions and issues with complex answers involving multiple points of view, they need to know how to find multiple documents that seldom appear neatly at the top of the hits returned for a single query. To do that, students need a more complex set of knowledge, skills, and attitudes. We tend to work with librarians and teachers who understand that their students are not getting what they would like them to get for their research purposes. We start with people who understand the importance of both precision and recall. With their help, we can try to develop tools that they can use with their students.

Are you at all concerned that it might be a very small part of the population that shares this interest and understands this problem?

I find myself thinking about that during the middle of the night. But it's also true that some people who seem unconcerned *do* understand the problem, and would have a greater interest in solving the problem if they had more confidence that they could do something about it. Sometimes it's not that they aren't concerned, but that they don't see a practical solution that will work for them. For us that's an important distinction. People who say, "Oh, of course it's important, but I really don't know what to do next" are an important audience for all of us who do care.

Our project goal is to ensure that every student has the opportunity to acquire 21st-century information fluency skills. But we know that we need to work with educators first. Librarians and teachers are the most critical links to helping students improve their information skills. So, we try to create learning materials, tools, and experiences that will work for both.

Have you faced any barriers in introducing either the skills or the specific interfaces that you've worked on?

The main barrier, as with all educators, is time. Many people will come to workshops and say, "this is a really important topic, I'd like to get involved, but I just don't feel like I have time. I'm the librarian, I'm covering seven periods a day, I can't get a substitute, teachers are busy." Time, I suppose, is the universal barrier. The other barrier is that teachers don't believe there's a tool that's going to solve this problem. They tend to be very skeptical about silver-bullet solutions. They know that this is really going to require learning on the part of the student, and they know that learning is going to take time. They shy away because they think it's going to be too time-consuming or impractical, not because they don't think it's important.

Is there also a sense that everybody can already search with proficiency? Do teachers and students seem to feel that they know the Web and are satisfied with good-enough information?

That's certainly something we encounter frequently; students in particular will say, "I'm already expert." It's one of the reasons assessment of 21CIF skills is so important. With assessments tools, we can say, "Great, if you're an expert, you can place out of this experience. Here are three search tasks. If you can complete them efficiently and effectively, you can begin your research or, better yet, help someone else improve their search skills. If you can't perform these tasks, then we'd like for you to understand why." The practice database I mentioned earlier is a learning tool with embedded assessments, and our micro-module learning experiences have embedded assessments as well. Integrating both formative and summative—that is, in-process and final—assessments is a critical element for success.

On the other side of that, as students use your interface and your databases, and make these discoveries, are they coming to some "ah-ha's"?

Here's an anecdote. We've acquired a lot of our information by sitting down with students and filming them as they go through a search, and then analyzing that experience, trying to break that down into the smallest pieces we possibly can. Then we look at what's different between those who are successful and unsuccessful with a particular search. I vividly remember going through a search with a student who eventually found the answer to the question, after about 30 minutes. I said, "Good for you, you found the answer." And she said, "Well, you know, I almost always do." She took a deep breath, sighed and said, "But it just takes me forever." And I said, "I think I could cut your search time on this particular search in half, if that would interest you." And she said, "Yeah." So I said, "If you learn to use the 'Find In This Page' command on your browser's toolbar, and if you know the keywords you're searching for, it could help you locate the text you need. I watched another student do this same search using the 'find' command and it took him about half the time, and after watching you do this search, I would be willing to bet if you did it again you could cut your search time in half."

I'm not saying that that would cut everybody's time in half, or cut her time in half on every query. But for most people, and most searches, there are strategies they could use that would make a significant difference. Librarians and teachers don't have time to do this with every student, but if we can identify a problem that wastes a student's time, provide a quick and effective tip, and provide them with a demonstration of improved results, most people will respond. My "ah-ha" in this instance was that I had to be able to do all three of these things to get her attention.

So we're trying to develop tools and experiences that address all these elements.

Strategies like using "find" don't take a lot of time to learn, but you can't assume that everybody knows this stuff. We need to get the word out about other powerful concepts that save searchers time and frustration.

I couldn't agree more. We also have to pay attention to efficiency. We've learned that the hard way. Our learning experiences for students of all ages have become shorter and shorter. Most recently we've developed online learning materials we call micro-modules. Micro-modules are very small, bite-size learning experiences. They start with a short set of multiple-choice questions, so you can self-assess to learn whether you know this already. They then provide a bite-sized learning experience about some aspect of searching, followed by a post-assessment that provides immediate feedback on what you learned. There are certain *gateway concepts*, the ones that open doors and make the most difference in the search experience. We now have about forty of them online. They are designed to introduce students to the concepts and strategies that might help them, and to enable them to use these strategies in a self-guided way. We're beginning to add audio and video components to make them more efficient and more responsive to different learning styles.

What are some examples of gateway concepts?

Understanding that one of the advantages of digital information resources is that they can be scanned quickly using the "find" command can open a door to thinking about searching differently. Another is understanding the difference between a natural language question and an effective search query. Another is understanding that information on the Internet isn't unorganized, it's just organized in different ways. What constitutes a gateway concept may be different for different people. We try to create a wide range of entry points so people can find a starting point that makes sense for them. For example, understanding why one-word queries are almost never very helpful can be a useful starting point for younger students. The average query, the last time I looked, was 1.8 words among the major search engines. So we know a lot of people are entering one-word queries. That's something you can address in an automated fashion. If someone enters a one-word query, you can give him or her some feedback saying that one-word queries rarely focus very well. Then refer them to a micro-module on query formation and see if they can focus a bit better.

To reach a large number of students, it saves time to do this in an automated way. But what a good teacher or librarian or peer counselor does is look for those gateway concepts that will make the most difference the quickest. That, I think, is what students find most motivating. If you give them 50 rules and the first three don't make a lot of difference, usually they're not going to hang in there. But if you give them three rules that make a difference instantaneously, then they're more likely to look for the next three.

You've been observing students with the benefit of both automated and human intrusion. Understand that I use "intrusion" in a positive way. Certainly the automated intrusion is scalable. Is there a difference in level of acceptance between automated and human?

We haven't done any hard research on this, although I'd like to. It's on our list of grants to write. But I know from looking at all sorts of computer-aided instruction that really good teachers are irreplaceable for their human interactions and their understanding of students and their caring for them. On the other hand, we also know that, for many students, automated feedback feels less critical and more objective, and allows them to feel that the locus of control remains with them.

I think that's important developmentally, especially with teenagers.

That sounds like the voice of experience. We work with middle school and high school students primarily, and I should emphasize that point. I'm not making generalizations that apply outside that group. But there are certainly instances in which we think automated feedback can be better for some students.

What differences have you noted in terms of age and readiness to perform certain tasks related to searching?

I don't have any real data about this issue but, on the basis of my own observations, I'd say the affective domain—a student's attitudes, beliefs, and values—is at least as important as the cognitive domain—a student's knowledge and intellectual skills. We've made the most headway by focusing on that. One developmental issue does come to mind, though. It has to do with dualistic thinking versus multifaceted thinking. According to William Perry's developmental scale [194]—Perry is a researcher who created a scale of intellectual development and some assessments to place people on the scale—dualistic thinking is characterized by the belief that there are right or wrong answers to things, rather than multiple answers to things. In the context of searching, an example would be the firm belief that there is a best search engine, as opposed to lots of good search engines useful for different things. With younger children, we may not be able to move beyond that stage of viewing the world. But with older learners, we would consider that attitude to be one that can be changed. If we can demonstrate that you can get better search results for some searches by using multiple search engines, for example, we can ask in a noncritical way whether it's always the best strategy to use your favorite search engine.

When you're working with students or designing interfaces that work with students, what kind of toolkit do you set up to help kids make these choices? Is there a toolkit that makes sense in terms of listing subject directories and search engines and, I'd think, subscription databases?

The answers are ever-changing, of course, as we continue to learn from our users. But we've set up our site with one-stop shopping in mind, because it saves time. We haven't yet achieved the complete suite that students want. We continue to work on that. The underlying principle is that the easier it is for students to pursue good search strategies, the more likely they are to adopt them. From the teacher's point of view, the more tools you have at hand, the easier it is to say, "I notice that you are trying to drive a nail, but you are using a screwdriver. See if you can find another tool that might be more useful to you." A real example might be constraining the search by domain. If students understand the concept that Web sites are organized into different domains by different types of organizations, this strategy will make sense to them. And yet if you say, "Now, go to your favorite search engine and search by domain," most people can't do it. They didn't know or have forgotten, and the help pages aren't always helpful, and so they simply don't do it. We found that, if we made it quicker and easier, students were more willing to adopt a better strategy. That's part of what good interfaces do; they make it easier for the student to follow an effective strategic path rather than an ineffective one. Really bad interfaces are those that encourage people to take really bad strategic paths. I won't mention any names …

That's probably wise.

To return to your earlier question about obstacles to helping students learn good search habits, the commercial search environment offers many opportunities for students to learn bad habits. Practice doesn't make perfect. Practice makes permanent. And many students are being encouraged to practice questionable search habits.

Let's talk about what "best practice" looks like. In terms of the portals and interfaces that have been developed by librarians or teachers or companies or organizations, what

does "good" look like? What's helpful to students and to adults and teachers?

That's a hard question because the answer depends so much on the purpose of the portal and the needs of the user. Our job as educators is to help students learn to align those two things. I would look for search sites that make their purpose clear, that encourage the use of multiple search strategies, that provide really useful online help, that provide tools to aid thinking, and that challenge students to learn while they are searching. Our search site isn't designed to provide the most powerful search tools, to compete with the big search sites. Our site is designed to provide learning tools. Our purpose is learning support, not performance support.

I'm going to back way up and ask you how you learned to search. How did you come to think about this stuff in a way that was effective?

How much time do you have? Searching is such an interesting topic for me because, at its core, it is a problem-solving process. As a result, it shares a great deal with the problem-solving methods used in science, mathematics, writing, social science, even art. Much has been written about these processes and we can learn from them all. But I just love solving problems. So, when I came to this problem called finding information, I attempted to use strategies I used for all problem solving, and discovered they worked. This started to dawn on me in graduate school, but didn't become really conscious until I started to teach it. I took a lot of science and math as an undergraduate, and then I studied humanities as a graduate student. In some ways I saw the connection just by sheer immersion. I might have discovered it earlier if someone had pointed it out to me. I had an "ah-ha" moment when I was introduced to Dialog [52]. I felt like I'd discovered a new world. I still had to solve search problems but it enabled me to do things so much more efficiently and effectively. I was hooked.

It's funny, everybody I'm interviewing is a fellow Dialog searcher. And everybody is remembering that "select sets" thing.

I can't resist telling you a story about Dialog. Recently I attended the 20th anniversary reunion of the first class I taught at the North Carolina School of Science and Mathematics. While we were sitting around chatting, not one, but two or three people came up to me and said, "Twenty years ago, when you were teaching us to use Boolean logic so we could search for things in Dialog, we were looking at each other, going, 'Why are we learning math in English class?' Now I get it."

For me it was just applying a generic process to a specific instance. I had a little early success that way, enough to keep me going and give me enough experience to get better. Now, when I think about helping others learn to search, I think of it in terms of generic problem solving, which is discipline-independent.

It's pretty wonderful when kids get these metacognitive "ah-ha's," like, "Oh yeah, this is important; I'm doing this right."

We can encourage more of that by encouraging more metacognitive thinking. Metacognitive thinking is one of the characteristics of expert searchers. Those "ah-ha" moments are not only learning moments, they are confidence-builders. We need materials and learning experiences and tools that encourage metacognitive, "ah-ha" moments. Integrated learning environments like those we're trying to develop can help to speed up that process of having repeated small successes that lead to more knowledge, that build a little more confidence, that lead to a little more patience, that encourage greater persistence. Before long the system is hitting on all cylinders. As we know, that's an important part of what good learning's about, and what good teachers do.

David, can you predict where the searching scene is going?
Some people say that we won't have to improve our
searching skills because search engines will get smarter.

I think they're getting incrementally better. I really, really appreciate that effort on the part of the researchers and builders. But I'm skeptical that they're going to make a quantum leap anytime soon. They are getting better at precision, and in certain specialized areas, like finding addresses and the like. But they're not getting better at recall-related issues. For all of us in education that's a really important distinction.

My views are probably influenced by the slow evolution of natural language processing over the past 20 years. Research in this area has led to steady, incremental improvements but not the breakthroughs predicted 20 years ago. Even if a breakthrough does occur, until then we will still need to focus on helping people learn to make the best use of the tools we have. At this point, we don't even come close. However much the tool is improved, it will still only be as good as the person's ability to use it. I don't think that equation ever changes.

What do you see as the role for the human guide with kids?
People argue that librarians are not needed as much
because kids have this great feeling of independence and
really are working at home. What do you see in your world?

You and I are in similar worlds; I see a lot of what you see. I do think that librarians, like teachers, need to learn to be guides by the side, not sages on the stage. When librarians serve as intermediaries, when a student asks a librarian to look up information and bring it back to them, that's equivalent to "giving someone a fish" in the old Chinese proverb. I believe librarians will increasingly need to become educators who teach people to fish.

I've described it, and heard it described, as transactional
versus transformational.

I like that terminology. There will always be a need for both, but the graph lines are going in different directions, one up and one down. Perhaps that's truer in school libraries than in public libraries. The Illinois School Library Media Association [80] published a set of standards for school librarians, called Linking for Learning [118], that describes the need for school librarians to take on a more proactive role as educators and to become transformation-oriented. I also believe that what's going to drive the change isn't technology, but people. Our students are, as you say, feeling increasingly empowered to do this kind of work at home, where there's no transactional help available. As they learn to do that more, I believe there'll be less and less demand for help of the transactional kind. I don't want to sound like a sage; this is speculation. But that's my best guess based on what I can see at this point.

Do you have any brilliant methods for motivating kids, teenagers especially, to be concerned about information quality and improving their searching skills?

Alas, I don't have any silver bullets. Our current answer to that question is to try to put power in the students' hands and say, show us how well you search. If you can demonstrate that you can locate, evaluate, and use information effectively enough to do the serious research we expect in all disciplines, we'll accept that. In fact, we'd like to know more about how you do it so we can share the information with others. If you can't, then we'd like to help you learn to search more effectively. If we can provide a context in which students see that as a responsibility to themselves and to their peers, rather than as a means of getting a grade, then it's more likely to make a real difference in their learning. At IMSA we are committed to making learning problem-centered, inquiry-based, standards-driven, and integrative. That's our educational philosophy. I'm convinced that if we steer students toward authentic problems that they care about, they are likely to be more motivated about learning in general. Our work with students and teachers regarding 21st-century information fluency reflects those beliefs. If learning becomes more important to students, becoming more information-literate and fluent will become important to them, too. That's my philosophical answer.

It makes a lot of sense to me. Staying philosophical, you did your graduate work in the humanities; how did that prepare you for the work you're doing now?

That's an interesting question. I have a PhD in English literature, but my undergraduate work was focused on science. Research is an important part of both of those worlds. I spent a few years in business and became interested computer technology. Once I started teaching, I worked in the computer industry as a programmer during the summers. I guess I was looking for ways to bring all these interests together. As it turns out, using technology in education was how that happened. Computers, like libraries, are places where many disciplines meet and co-exist and sometimes even cross-pollinate.

So, you are a Renaissance man, David.

I wouldn't say that, unless you mean old. I do qualify for that. It's true that I'm interested in the space where different disciplines and ideas meet. Searching is also a process where that happens. My interest in searching is deeply rooted in my interest in language and technology. I've learned most of what I've learned by just doing things. I got into all this early enough that you could get away with that.

Searching for me is not all serious and academic, it's also fun. It enhances our ability to learn and to shine lights into dark places. That's what I think ultimately motivates students, giving them a sense of the power of learning. Risky as it may be, I think it's worth saying: learning *should* be fun.

Super Searcher Power Tips

➤ Use keywords appropriate to the topic you are searching. When we search, we tend to select keywords that we would use to describe what we're looking for. But every subject matter has its particular language. Scientists use scientific language. Artists use the language of art. If you can find that language, you have a better chance of matching documents on any particular topic.

➤ Use the browser's Find command. Much of the time we spend searching is actually spent looking through Web pages to see if they contain the information we need. The Find command enables us to scan a document quickly for search terms or for related terms.

➤ Vary your focus. Once we've selected search terms, it's easy to stay locked into that focus and miss many documents related to your topic. Expert searchers know how to vary the focus of their search by using both more specific and more general terms.

➤ Search the Invisible Web. The most popular search engines are designed to search for static Web pages. Many useful sites, including government sites such as the Library of Congress, generate their pages dynamically from their own databases. As a result, search engines don't include them in their indexes. Remember that many of the most useful databases for education aren't on the free Web at all.

➤ Think out of the searchbox. We tend to think of search-ing as entering keywords in the searchbox of a search engine and looking at the results. But finding what we're looking for is often best achieved by using other tools, like the site map of a promising Web site, or the specialized search engine provided on a site, or the table of contents or headers on a page. As with most problem solving, it's important when searching to fit the tool to the task.

Deb Logan

Finding the Marbles, Opening the Geodes (Helping Learners Understand Through Story)

At Mount Gilead High School in Ohio, Deb Logan is librarian/media specialist and information goddess, and is resource person for both students and teachers. Deb is the author of *Information Skills Toolkit: Collaborative Integrated Instruction for the Middle Grades* [190, see Appendix] and co-author of *K–12 Web Pages: Planning and Publishing Excellent School Web Sites* [191]. She is a member of Ohio's Technology Academic Content Standards and Ohio's Guidelines for Effective School Library Media Programs writing teams [139]. She is active in the Ohio Educational Library Media Association [81] and is a frequent speaker at professional conferences.

jd3logan@bright.net
www.deblogan.com

What fascinates you about searching, Deb?

Initially, my interest was due to my desire to teach our students to "manage" the Web. Once I got started with searching, I immediately enjoyed the process. It reminds me of doing reference work. I approach reference work like a puzzle. I have to figure out what I really need and then decide where I am likely to find my answer. That is when the fun—the search—begins. Being able to find the answer is satisfying on several levels. Solving the puzzle is personally rewarding and also gives me credibility among the faculty and students. Teachers, students, and recently even a few parents have told me, "You can find anything."

My first searching experiences were when I volunteered to become a KidsConnect [121] volunteer through AASL's

ICONnect [111]. KidsConnect was designed to have professional school librarians electronically assist students to become better users of the Internet. Students would e-mail homework questions, and librarians would construct pathfinders that basically walked students through finding information online. The specificity of the pathfinder would depend on the age level of the students requesting assistance. It was actually a teaching process. The pathfinders were designed to help students think about what they were really looking for, where they were likely to find it, and how to evaluate sources and information. With the younger kids, we were more likely to actually take them to the right answer. With the older kids, we would make it possible for them to understand how to find high-quality information themselves, through a logical path.

So KidsConnect introduced you to searching. Did it change the way you taught?

I went through KidsConnect training in the summer of 1997. Before I started my training, I knew that there were wonderful and lousy things on the Web. I also knew that the school in which I taught was literally and figuratively on the wrong side of the tracks. My students did not have computers at home and were not likely to have them in the near future. The computers that were being placed in our library were the only ones to which they were likely to have access. I wanted two things. I wanted to teach them to search the Internet and to find a way to mine the best of the Web for our middle school kids. And I wanted to put together a Web site that would direct them to things that would support and enrich the curriculum and meet some of their informational needs. I was not just doing this for my students. Most of the teachers in that school did not have a computer at home, and we were looking toward eventually having a computer in each classroom. I wanted to assist the teachers and the students. I participated in KidsConnect because I felt it was a valuable service and an invaluable opportunity for me to learn how to use the Internet. After KidsConnect, I was able to take an intermediate level graduate class on Internet searching from Kent State University's library school.

Since I was a middle school librarian, I answered middle school questions for KidsConnect. Many of those questions aligned with our curriculum. While doing volunteer work, I was going out on the Web and finding great sources. This was not only fun and helpful to the online students, many of the sites I found became part of the foundation for my own school Web site. The first year the site was up, in June 1999, *School Library Journal* [175] named it the site of the month.

Very cool. Can you talk a bit about how your Web site contributes to instruction in terms of searching?

It has a "Things to Know About the Internet" page. That page talks about Web basics such as Boolean logic, and about how to evaluate Web information. My now-defunct search engine page was also a teaching tool. Directories, true search engines, and metaengines were grouped into categories along with explanations describing the differences between them and with hints for when to use which one. I have had several different pages with links to bogus Web sites. They are effective teaching tools. If students experience being fooled by particular Web sites, the lesson has more credibility than simply telling them that there is inaccurate information on the Web. It is also a fun activity.

Can you describe one activity that helps students learn searching skills while they're doing other things?

I have a lesson that I would love to share with you. I use it to remind students to use their search skills before turning them loose to work on a research project. It involves an approximately 3-foot-tall glass jar that looks like an oversize canning jar. It is filled with grains of rice, and I have stuck some marbles in the jar so the students can see the marbles up and down the sides of the jar. A smaller clear canister is also filled with rice and a few marbles. A third, very small, clear container is loaded with marbles and beautiful crystal. A few grains of rice are scattered in the smallest container.

The lesson starts with the huge jar. The students are intrigued by the rice jar and *want* to know what it is. I ask them how they think the jar might relate to an Internet search. After a class discussion, the students invariably decide that the grains of rice are unwanted Web sites found by a search engine and the marbles are the good stuff. When I agree with them, I suggest they think about search engine results pages. When you get a screen of hits, you usually get a list of 10 Web pages at a time. I have the students imagine taking the grains of rice out of this jar 10 grains at a time to get to the marbles. They do not like that idea. We then talk about how we could get to the good stuff more quickly.

One of the first lessons I do with students is on keyword strategies. Students almost immediately reply, "You could be more specific." I respond by bringing out the mid-size jar. We talk about using specific language and playing with a lot of different words until we discover ones that fit what we want to find and we start getting better search results. I ask the students, "*But do you really still want to go through all these grains of rice to get to the marbles?*" The room resounds with the word "No!" I then ask them, "What could we do to have a more effective search?" The students respond that we should use Boolean logic.

Then I show them the smallest clear container filled with the "good stuff." We review the value of utilizing advanced search techniques, Boolean logic, and specific words to get to the good stuff. When you get to the good stuff, you still may have some rice in there, but not as much.

Finally, I show the students a geode. Initially, a geode looks like a plain rock. When split open, it reveals a hollow cavity and the inner walls are lined with crystals. The insides look like a treasure! I found my geode at a festival where it was split open right in front of me. I was able to keep both halves. They can usually be found in nature-type stores. I tell my students how I obtained my geode and that the cost of the rock depended on the color-coded marks on the outside. We talk about the people who mark the geodes being experts, or at least making an educated guess about what is inside of each rock based on what they know about rocks. I have left the green code marks on it. I tell the students, in order to know which of the plain-looking rocks I wanted to pay money for, I looked at the markings on the outside. Then I open the geode and reveal the insides to my students. I ask the students if it would be helpful to read the descriptions and make decisions about which hits you want to open before looking at search results. By using available clues in the descriptions, a searcher can save time and find the good stuff quicker.

You make learning very tangible, Deb. Do kids remember your lessons?

Oh, yes. I started this lesson during my third year at this school. I first presented it before the senior research project got underway. Students looked at me and I could see light bulbs going on. And I said "*Now* do you see the reason for the Boolean logic?" Later in the year, they would teach the lesson to teachers, who then came into the library with their research groups and asked about the jars of rice.

This is a rural school system. My instruction basically provides the first lessons in information literacy that my students experience. Perhaps five students in the high school had even heard of Google [15] when I began teaching there. Students knew Yahoo! [43], AskJeeves [4], and maybe Dogpile [8], but that was it. When I first taught Boolean logic, it was easy to see some of the kids getting it, but I had to really work on selling it because they were used to just floundering around without any strategies. The teachers and I have seen remarkable changes in how students search and conduct research. There is no question that they are more effective, but they still have a long way to go.

With a lot of the search engines assuming an AND operator now, do you use the advanced search screens when you

**teach about Boolean? Do you use the databases? How do
you prove this stuff to students?**

My lesson on Boolean logic involves pizza toppings and partners. It is one that helps students easily visualize and understand
Boolean logic. It is followed by an activity in which students use
Boolean logic to find Web sites related to teaching math concepts. I want the students to understand that advanced searching is doing math with words. I have gotten most of the students
to the point where they start searching by automatically opening
up the advanced search screen. Many do not bother with the
opening screen now.

And they see the power in this?

Yes, they do. That first year, very few did. Once I managed to
sell some of the students, and they really figured out what was
happening, those students were the best advocates. They went
around and taught each other. Now I also have a reputation
among the teachers and students for being able to find anything.
That helps my credibility, too. My biggest problem the first year
was the mindset that once they had been in the library for an ori-
entation, that was it; there was nothing more I would be able to
teach them.

**But you discovered that wasn't true. Was high school a little
intimidating?**

When I started working at this level, there was no question
that I was a little scared, because I have always worked with
younger students. Now, I am having a wonderful time. I enjoy
working with high school students because I can reason with
them.

I have a lesson that I am using now with freshmen to help
them understand how their knowledge of information literacy
evolves. It also helps the students develop constructive criticism
skills for peer editing and group process skills. I have put
together sets of eight clip-art pictures of bicycles, from a Big

Wheel all the way through to a motorbike. Each group of students gets a set of cards and a different task. On a big piece of paper, they have to write their task at the top. One task is "Put the pictures in order." Another task is listing how many ways you could put them in order. A third asks the students to list similarities, while the fourth asks for differences. A fifth is only used with large groups and has students brainstorm, "What do these pictures have to do with learning?" The students brainstorm and write down their ideas, using flip chart markers. We do a gallery walk with sticky notes. They love being handed those packets of sticky notes. The groups rotate around the room contributing feedback to the other groups' answers and ideas.

When they return to their own table, each of the groups decides what feedback they are going to use and what they are not going to use. They conclude by reporting back to the class as a whole. I follow up by asking the class how the picture sets relate to learning. When the students come up with "starting with the easiest and working up to the hardest," I say, "I would like you to stop a minute and think about the following statement. A lot of people think that when you have been to the library once, you know what you need to do and there is not really anything else you can learn." I usually see a roomful of heads nodding in agreement with this statement. I follow it by asking, "Would you like me to have the expectations for your projects in ninth grade that I have for the senior projects? Or do you think there are some things you might need to learn between now and then?" The group members invariably vehemently respond with a "yes" to that question. After that, I make the point that the bicycles all have wheels, pedals, and handlebars. Then I pull out an information literacy model and show that, as with the bicycles, there are basic steps that are part of any research process. The basics are important and you have to know how to use them before you move to more sophisticated bicycles—or research projects. When students come into the library for research, they need to watch for the differences in how we expect them to do research as their skill levels increase. We expect they will grow and become more sophisticated users of information. Each time we meet, our goal is to take their work up to a higher level.

And they get that?

They get that. I reinforce it by giving them another set of task cards. One table gets math, the second table gets science, the third table gets language arts, and the fourth table gets social studies. If there is a fifth group, they are given a list of special classes—art, music, and physical education. I then have the groups brainstorm how, just like with the bicycle and the library, there are foundations, and there are things that change over time, in the different subject areas. For example, in language arts you start with letters, then you go to words, to picture books, chapter books, and then novels. For math, they might list that they use addition in general math, in algebra, in trigonometry, and in calculus. They quickly figure out that they are really glad that, although they use addition through-out their education, they do not start out using it to do calcu-lus. Ultimately, it is a lesson in metacognition about how people learn.

Whenever you can create a picture in a kid's mind it works pretty well. Deb, what do you want your students to be able to do before they leave your doors?

I want them to know the difference between a subscription database and the free Web. I want them to be aware that they are more likely to be successful if they do not go into a search with a "locked vocabulary"—using *one* word or *one* phrase, and expect-ing that "my word" is always going to get exactly what they want; I want them to have keyword strategies. I want them to think like we did pre-Web. Before the Web, if I wanted medical informa-tion, I would go to a doctor. If I wanted information about melanoma, I would contact the American Cancer Society. Instead of just searching for melanoma willy-nilly with a search engine, go to the American Cancer Society [78] Web site, or another reputable source for medical information like the Mayo

Clinic [129] Web site, and look for melanoma there. Ask the expert. You do not have to just take the potluck of what you find on the Web. If you are looking for something about panda bears, I know that the National Zoo [133] is likely to have good material on panda bears, or links to good information. Expert Web sites might not have definitive information, but they are likely to have reliable information that searchers probably will not find elsewhere on the free Web. So think and then go.

Another thing I want is for them to really be specific about what they're looking for. One of the things I tell students is that any person you can think of is smarter than the fastest, best computer in the world. Computers can only do what they are programmed to do. We are not there yet with artificial intelligence. Using natural language is still far from being as effective as thinking about keywords and creating a Boolean search. I also want students to really understand how advanced searches work and what they mean.

It sounds like you're not trusting the search engines and the databases to get smart enough to understand our casual or natural language searches.

Oh, I think they will, but search tools are not there yet. I like to teach kids to be flexible. Right now on my dry-erase board I have written "Yes, you know Google, but have you tried ..." and I list about 10 tools including KartOO [22], HotBot [19], WiseNut [42], Vivisimo [39], and About.com [2]. They love the look of KartOO. I do not want them to be in a rut. I want them to know that, if at first you do not succeed, try a different search tool. The last time I read statistics on what percentage of the Web Google covers, it was about 40 percent.

I heard it was even less, and I found that shocking. But it's likely true, when you think about what really is and isn't on the Invisible Web.

The Invisible Web is probably growing faster than the visible Web right now. And Google doesn't even touch that, for all intents and purposes. Because our filter blocks images on Google, I send students to HotBot for image searches. You can specify the format—images, PDF, Real Audio, video, and others.

Deb, do you do much in terms of faculty in-service?

I have done some in-service training in the past. Also, when I collaborate with teachers, they hear what I am teaching their students. Often they express interest in my teaching them a workshop, and that is something I would like to do. In this district there is a technology director and a person in charge of technology training. Training is supposed to go through them, and we have repeatedly talked about my doing some training. They have expressed interest, but it has only actually happened a handful of times.

What barriers do you face?

The main one is the student, the "I know it all already" mindset that we discussed earlier. We have a student whose father owns one of the Internet service providers in our area. His family business provides Internet access to a large number of people. One day he said, "Mrs. Logan, I know you're teaching today, and I just don't think you can teach me anything." I said, "Well, I bet you can teach me some things, and there might be one or two things I can teach you." On his way out of class he said, "You win." I replied, "No, we both win. I definitely can learn from you."

Part of the problem is that, by the time they get to me, they have some habits that are hard to break. They should stop thinking in terms of natural language. Although I like a few, I am not a big fan of metaengines. I would like to see students move beyond Dogpile and AskJeeves. With our system, sometimes Web pages are "trapped" in the AskJeeves frames. This impedes my efforts to have students cite sources.

They can't really see where documents are coming from.

Exactly! Students can get wrapped up in surfing, bouncing around without actually stopping to use the information.

Searching can be just a plaything; they sometimes bounce-bounce-bounce-bounce around pages without using information. When I first suggested that students try KartOO, there were a couple of boys who spent all of their time "playing" KartOO and not gathering information. Ultimately, they did their project, but their time in the library was not productive.

Deb, when you search on your own, what are your favorite tools?

I have had extremely good luck with About.com. I like their experts, and I also like that some of the experts have mailing lists that keep me up-to-date on specific topics. I subscribe to some of those. I like that About.com clearly identifies sponsored links. I try to encourage my students to use About.com, not just for its links, but because sometimes they can find useful original information there. One time we had searched extensively for an esoteric disease. We could not find anything until we searched it on About.com. The About.com expert was a physician who had written a series of About.com Web pages about that specific disease. It was the proverbial goldmine.

About.com works really well for a lot of popular topics, as well as some educational ones. Most kids would never think to use that one even if we linked to it.

Success sells, especially when your peers are finding exactly what they need. I have had good luck with getting kids to use it. I also like Internet Public Library [21]. When I am starting a search for links to reliable information, that is one of the places I go first. I like it because professionals with exacting standards have culled and annotated the best of the Web. When I build a "project page" of recommended links for a research project, I find links on IPL that lead to other good links.

I use Google frequently, because I know how to "make it sing." When I use the advanced search feature, I almost always find what I want. Obviously, there are some areas where Yahoo! cannot be beaten. I use the directory features every day. If I want to know what movie is in town or across in the next county, I go to the Yahoo! movie database. I keep an eye on the Yahoo! newsbox during the day. It is usually where I first become aware of major news stories; several times it has alerted me to major new virus threats.

A combination use of search tools can be extremely effective. On September 11 one of our teacher's sons was in a building very close to the World Trade Towers. As soon as I found out about her concern, I asked her for the name of the building. I used Google to get the address of the building and then I used Yahoo! to get a map. Within five minutes, I had printed out a map and was able to show her how many blocks away it was. By starting with a search engine and then continuing with a directory, I was quickly able to help alleviate her concerns after she had fretted needlessly for hours.

There's a real power in combining your search tools. Each one might do a different thing well, and understanding which does what is incredibly useful. Shifting gears, let me ask about subscription services. Do you have any favorites?

We have EBSCOhost [53]. This year I am having a tremendous amount of success getting our students to use it. The seniors in particular are seeing its usefulness. Our senior government teacher values having our students learn information literacy skills. He wants his students to become strong users of information. He has devoted a tremendous amount of class time to getting the students in the library and having me work with them. One of the neat, neat things about that is that he is highly respected by our students. I think because he puts such credence in what I do, my capital with the seniors has risen unbelievably. Part of his final was for the students to list the three most valuable things that happened in the class. Several of the students mentioned what they had learned in the library. It was awesome. I feel like we are sending the seniors out with some really strong information skills.

Any other searching tricks you want to share?

With Boolean logic I like to use a restaurant analogy. You pick your restaurant based on what you are hungry for; you pick a search engine based on what you need. You read the menu, and think about what you want. You may even ask a friend for advice before ordering. Before you search, you pick your keywords based on what you want. When I teach students about keywords, I suggest that they ask a friend to help brainstorm possible keywords. I call it wordstorming.

That's a great term; I love it.

In the restaurant, you order exactly what you want. I want a sandwich. It has to have pickles. No tomatoes. I want it on whole wheat bread and I want it well done. And if it is wrong, you do not settle for it. You send it back and you try a different one. When you are searching, if it is wrong, you try different words to describe what you want. You do not settle for the wrong thing.

I really like the way you offer students clear mental pictures. One of the problems with the Web is that we can't imagine it well. Do you have any strategies for describing the concept of relevance? I don't think most kids think about relevance and how it works.

I try to emphasize to the students that search engines are there to make money. Searchers need to be aware of, and look at, why results appear in the order they do. I do try to find concrete examples, things that students can wrap their minds around and things that make learning meaningful to them. For me, that is best practice. When I teach something, I want to see light bulbs go on. When a student is stuck with a search and needs help, I want their hands on the computer and I want the solution to the problem to be something I help them find based on what they already know. I want them to think about what it is they really need. Is this a directory or a search engine question? Is this an EBSCOhost-type question? Learning is doing and thinking as opposed to being told.

So what does a good searcher look like?

A good searcher goes into her search knowing what she wants, and is not willing to settle for less than "the good stuff." A good searcher goes in with more than one way of looking at her subject. A good searcher goes in knowing more than one way, knowing the kinds of searches that are possible, the different kinds of search tools and how they work. She is familiar with more than one of each kind of search tool. A good searcher knows how to structure a search within the different search tools. She knows to read the help page and see whether it is a plus sign, a capital A-N-D, or a default AND. She knows whether or not the search tool will accept parentheses or quotation marks for phrases.

I want my students to become, and then know that they are, powerful users of information. This effort starts during our library orientations. I tell my students that they will be working in an information society and that their ability to use information could impact their financial futures. I tell them that my goal is for them to be successful and that I will do my best to help them become expert users of information. I also let them know that I am looking forward to their coming back in a fancy car and taking me out for lunch—and we are not talking about the local pizza joint. While we all chuckle and grin about the car and lunch, we all know that I am serious about helping them become information-literate.

Super Searcher Power Tips

➤ Think and then do: Know what you need.

➤ Have a wordstorm! Brainstorm different ways to say what you need.

➤ Take along a friend—or a teacher, a librarian, or reference book—and ask for help with search terms.

➤ Call an expert. Think pre-Internet—*Whom* would you call? Go to the Source.

➤ Why settle for less? Hold out for what you *really* want.

➤ Look at who's talking. Are they qualified to talk about the topic?

Alice Yucht
Searching as Metaphor

Alice Yucht recently retired after 40 years as a school librarian. She now teaches an online school library/media programs and services course at Rutgers University's Graduate School of Communication, Information and Library Studies—a course she says is "otherwise known as 'so you really want to be a school librarian.'" Yucht actively speaks and writes on school library management issues.

Alice@aliceinfo.org
www.aliceinfo.org
http://aliceinfo.squarespace.com/blog

Alice, how long have you been searching?

Online, you mean? Let's see, I'm 60 years old. I've been searching the Web for at least 15 years, starting with an AOL account.

And you've been teaching searching for a while, too. You must have a few cool stories.

One that sticks with me is this: Once, when I asked a class to explain the difference between an index and a search engine, one clever lad replied that "indexes sort it out in advance and tell you what they have and where it is, but search engines have to be told what to look for, and then you have to hope they find what you want!"

He understood that you have to be a smarter searcher when you use a search engine. Do all your students have that same level of understanding?

Actually, no. I worry. Kids seem to think that if they put any-thing in a search box, an answer will come back. They need to understand that it has to do with being able to develop a ques-tion first. They're so used to the "infoglut" that they're willing to accept any answer that shows up—and it's not necessarily an answer that is useful. One of the things that bothers me when I watch kids searching is they'll stop at the sixth thing, because that's as far as the screen goes, and they don't think they have to go further.

If the best result is result number 300, they may never see that. How do we help them move wonderful result 300 up the list?

I explain to classes that there's a difference between some-thing that gets a number of hits versus something that's really useful. To make that point, several years ago I put up a Web page that said Heritage Middle School. That's all it said. And it said it a hundred times—just those three words. I said to the kids, do a search for Heritage Middle School. Of course the one I created would always come up first. Sometimes I would change it; some-times it would have a silly graphic on it. But all it said on the actual page was Heritage Middle School. It just kept popping up to the top. Then I'd say, scroll down in the page and show me what's in there that's useful.

That's a clever idea and a very clear lesson. Did they get the concept you were hoping they'd get?

Yes, then they would get it.

As a veteran teacher-librarian, when the information literacy standards came out in the form of *Information Power* [186, see Appendix], was it like a Ten Commandments for you?

Did you already have an instinctive idea of what you should be teaching?

In 1988, it didn't have as much of an impact because it was idealistic. I almost had the feeling it had been written by people who hadn't worked in a real school library. But in '98, it seemed much closer to reality. The second edition of *Information Power*, what we call IP2, meshed rather well with what I believed I should be teaching. It was almost as a scope and sequence. It also gave me the documentation I needed, almost an imprimatur, to say to administrators, "Look, I'm not just talking off the top of my head. This comes from two national, well-recognized organizations; they are saying 'this is what our kids should be able to accomplish.' We're not able to accomplish it the way we're doing it now." One of the reasons is the chasm between the classroom teacher and the librarian. The classroom teacher is told to use technology, but given very little guidance as to how to use it. The librarian is saying, "You're throwing students at me telling me what they 'need,' but you have no clear foundation for knowing how they should learn it."

In terms of searching, that chasm seems to be huge, doesn't it? Now that everyone can get *some* good results for themselves, perhaps the idea that there's more to learn about searching is less obvious to students and their teachers.

I'll give you an interesting example. I used to do workshops for student teachers in my building. One of them was on how to find the best Web resources for your class. The workshops weren't required; it was always interesting to see who did and didn't show up. Women showed up, men didn't. It had no correlation to the subject areas they were teaching. I don't know if I can make a generalization about gender here, except that the men seemed to think that it was technology and they knew what they were doing. The women were more willing to ask for help.

I did talk to each of the student teachers as I got to them and asked how I could help them, what could I do to make it better. Inevitably, from the women I would get, "Well, I've been told to use this and I'm really not sure… So, yeah, I'm willing to accept any help I can get." The men would say, "Well, I'm very busy, you know. I'm coaching this, I'm doing that …" There was always an excuse. Interestingly, the guys most willing to ask for help were in the sciences.

One in particular—a young punk, for want of a better word—came in, marched himself over to the computer during his prep period. He was using Google. I asked if I could help with anything. "No," he said, "I'm fine." So I walked away. He was busy searching and searching, and I could see that he was starting to look a little frustrated, so I went back and said, "You're working in so-and-so's class, right? What unit are you doing now?"— knowing full well what unit it was. He said, "Well, she wants me to do a unit on Australia, so I thought I'd find a Web site that the whole class could go to, and I'd give them a list of questions to answer." I asked, "Oh, did you find anything?" He said, "Yeah, I got this great site. Look, it's got pictures and everything." I looked at it, and it said Angelfire.

So he wasn't aware that a free hosted site like Angelfire might be less than authoritative? What did you do?

I pointed out that we have a number of books on Australia, and he responded, "I don't want to waste time with books because they won't have the really good stuff." I asked him what kind of questions he was going to ask, and he said, "You know, the usual, 'what's the capital?' and all that." I tried pointing out that we had all these other resources and that there were lots of ways to approach this. But even after all his fruitless searching, he insisted, "I don't have time. I just need to get my students in and out." I thought to myself, I'm not going to say anything, because obviously he doesn't want help. He scheduled the class not to come to the library, but to go to the computer lab. He said to the computer lab person, who is also a teacher, "Could you just bookmark this site on all the computers?" He handed her the URL and she said no.

It sounds like some folks coming out of teacher prep programs don't have a clue that librarians are information professionals, or that we might play a role in helping them as student teachers.

That's the point; they don't. We librarians have to make sure they get that information. The younger ones, who consider themselves extremely computer-savvy, think they know it all and don't need any help. But they can't teach their kids how to search because they haven't really learned how to search themselves.

And it looks like their models of what a good site is are not what we expect learners to look for. What do you view as essential strategies for teaching searching?

Pre-research activities. By that I mean that the teacher needs to sit down with the class before they even start searching and not just develop essential questions, but ask them to consider the search terms they are most likely to be using. What are we really looking for? What kinds of information do I expect you to find? How do I expect you to use that information? In other words, there's got to be some advance preparation done by the teacher with the librarian, and by the teacher with the class.

Because it doesn't come intuitively to most kids.

We're hoping eventually it will, but not every kid is going to college, and not every kid understands all of it. Unfortunately, I see an interesting continuum, working backward, and I've worked on all the grade levels. High school teachers in large part think they should be teaching on the university level. Especially if they're teaching AP courses, they design assignments that go for the gold. And they always feel that the middle school people did not prepare these kids for high school. Middle school teachers tend to see that we're dealing with kids who are constantly in flux. They're going through all kinds of growth patterns that are physical, emotional, cognitive—everything—and even if you taught it to them yesterday, they may not have heard it. You have to give them a solid foundation on the middle school level because they probably didn't get it in elementary school. The elementary school teachers tend to do a far more structured "here is exactly where you're going and what you need to find." We must teach kids that before they start looking they must have some idea of what they're looking for.

It's funny; that idea comes up with everyone I interview.

When I'm teaching search strategies, I always include documentation because, as I tell students, "I don't want to know just that you looked and found it, I want to know *where* you found it. And I'm going to go check your sources just because I'm really mean and nasty. And I don't want to see Google [15] or AskJeeves [4] in your bibliography." I use analogies to help students understand that concept: "If I were to ask you where you bought those sneakers, would you point me to the mall map? A search engine is a mall map. No, I want to know what *store*."

The nice thing about that analogy is that when you're looking at the mall map you've already decided what you're shopping for. If you're looking for sneakers, you're not looking for cards. You're not looking for the food court. You've already made some decisions.

Certainly these planning strategies are cognitive issues. Are there also attitudinal issues that need to be addressed if students are going to search more effectively?

Yes, certainly! One of the attitude issues that we need to address is that mediocrity is acceptable. Somebody I know referred to it as the "American Idol" syndrome. That means being happy to accept the best of the worst. We don't know who was better but didn't try out for *American Idol*. It's the same rationale as why Lee Iacocca never ran for president. If you aren't careful you'll never know how much quality you are missing.

That makes sense. Are there other attitudinal issues we need to work on?

Willingness to put in the time. It's not just a question of payback. In some cases teachers are willing to accept mediocrity. Students don't have enough self-pride. But mostly, it's a "hurry up and get it over" syndrome. It's even more the case now that mediocrity is so readily available. I would also like to find a way to slow the scroll button. When I stand behind kids and see them scrolling up and down, I think, "No human being can possibly read that quickly." It's clicker mentality, like using the TV remote control—dismissing something without spending time to examine it carefully. Children have very short attention spans, some of it a direct result, unfortunately, of "Sesame Street," where everything happens in 60- or 90-second bites. Many kids have the attitude that "If I don't find it here, I'll just keep clicking. I don't know where I'm going, but I'm clicking, so I'm doing something."

Don't you think that if we give them some strategies, such as avoiding free hosting sites like Angelfire and many other personal sites, we could deal with the mediocrity issue pretty effectively? You can probably dismiss really bad results fairly quickly, and you can probably learn to recognize good stuff quickly, too.

Yes. But students have to be taught, and in a way that makes them think it's their own idea. You can't just dump an idea on them and say, "Look, you're going to do this," especially on the upper middle and high school level. There's a real sense of rebellion there. "Just 'cause the teacher said it, I'm not gonna do it"— unless there is some buy-in for the student.

One of the buy-ins could be that these behaviors are grade-dependent. You find truly good stuff, you're going to get an A.

Yes, and I picked that up from one of your workshops. You shared that your students' bibliographies had to be annotated. It was an "ah-ha!" And the teachers loved it. But it also meant to the kids that we were not just looking at what they'd looked at— they already knew I was the nasty type who would take their bibliography and say, "Uh, excuse me; I tried to find this site, but it didn't work"—but now they had to put some qualitative decision making into their choices. The premise I used when I introduced annotations was, "I'm going to look at what you're handing in as your bibliography because I'm always looking for good stuff to put into the pathfinders that I do. So if you come across something that's really super, I need to know about it. I'm going to *use* your stuff."

You're validating the importance of their search for quality. It gives student work an authentic audience, and some importance beyond the assignment. So, annotation is effective, in terms of searching instruction. What *else* works?

Well-designed pathfinders that take kids to quality sources. My definition of a pathfinder is a Web site that provides links to the most useful online resources for a specific curriculum. It includes online resources of all sorts, databases and so on, preselected by the librarian in collaboration with the teacher, to facilitate searching for a particular project.

The pathfinder may be structured in a way that requires students to go in steps. For example, I may put general stuff at the top, and then link to subtopics. The teacher may want them to go in a certain progression. I want them to learn how to scroll down. So I'll put stuff further down that they're going to have to find later. Unless I see stuff on your bibliography that you could only have gotten by using our pathfinder, your grade goes down.

That makes the pathfinder meaningful to a student, doesn't it?

It does. But some still need to be convinced. When the class was in the library, I found myself walking around saying, "You can do your own scattered searching at home. But in the library you're going to do what I call strategic searching, meaning I already set this stuff up for you; it has some serious value."

Part of our problem is that this same hurry-up mentality extends to teachers who don't want their students to "waste time searching." Some teachers don't want to take the time to set up the parameters. Best practice is really indicated by much more collaboration between teacher and librarian. It's saying, "Let's do a lot of the advance work together, and *we* decide what we want the kids to be looking for and learning." Best practice also means teachers who are actively involved in supervising and monitoring what their kids are doing while they're searching.

It's interesting that you focus on teachers, rather than teacher-librarians. I think that's essential. The pathfinders are important, but really, it's the teacher valuing these process skills that will make them important to learners.

I saw this very clearly last year with two social studies teachers who had very different attitudes about how the search process was going to happen. They were teaching the same unit. I was using the exact same pathfinder for both sets of classes. The difference was that one teacher spent the time while his kids were searching, walking back and forth, looking over their shoulders, asking what they'd found, talking about what they'd found, guiding them as needed. The other teacher said, "Go find what you need," and sat and marked papers. The students of that teacher would come up to me with their questions, and after a while I started to say, "I can help you find stuff but I can't always help you interpret it. You need to ask your teacher about that."

So you engaged him that way?

Right. But he was not happy. He saw the library period as prep time for him. He was there in body but not in mind.

I'm wondering about the importance of this over-the-shoulder style teaching. You're responding to individual problems as they occur rather than a general, "I'm teaching

you this but I don't know if it will ever come up in your lifetime of searching needs." For me, that immediate problem solving seems to be a valuable way of learning.

Yes, and the effect is even greater because the teacher is involved in the process. Students know that the teacher is watching what they're doing, and curious about and interested in what they're finding.

The other thing is that this type of teaching echoes the questioning that should go on in the kid's own brain. When you do that over-the-shoulder stuff, you're modeling and validating the kind of thinking skills that you hope the kids will develop independently.

That's the whole point. It models the thinking process.

Let's shift gears and talk a bit about some of your favorite specific search tools. What works for middle school learners?

I always start with the online subscription databases. In middle school, we use eLibrary [55] heavily, because it has the broadest range—newspaper and magazine articles, transcripts of TV and radio programs, plus lots of multimedia clips, graphics, and maps. Because we do a lot of social studies projects, I also highlight the ABC-CLIO [50] databases, which have an enormous range of primary sources plus background information originally published in print. These databases provide content that has been prevetted for quality and curriculum-relevant usefulness, and are constantly being updated. I don't have to worry about whether the information is just some kook's personal ravings.

What we're paying for is access to an enormous range of authoritative material that it would be impossible for us to access or provide any other way, or even have the shelf-space to store. Once students realize that using these databases means that they will *always* find useful information for their projects, they're less likely to waste time wading through all the untested stuff on the free Web. There's a reason these databases cost money; they provide a consistent level of quality materials in a single, easy-to-search package. Sending students to the subscription databases is important for that whole return-on-investment issue: use it or lose it. If I want to be able to keep supplying these quality resources, I've got to demonstrate why they're valuable so that teachers will incorporate them into their activities in the future.

How do you help your students understand all their search choices—the free Web, the databases? Do you believe kids need illustrations to help them get their arms around concepts like the differences between search engines, subject directories, and subscription services?

I use a lot of analogies to help students understand. It's about teaching kids to be critical consumers. More and more of them have disposable income, and they've started to figure out how and where to spend their money. I use a lot of analogies to help students understand. For the past six years I worked in an upper middle class community. These kids had no trouble understanding the difference between a big department store and the local Everything's-a-Dollar outlet. I asked them, "If you were invited to the White House and you needed something really special to wear, are you more likely to ask the clerk at Kmart or the sales associate at Nordstrom to help you?" This works for both boys and girls. Students would look at me like, "Why would you even set foot in Kmart?" And I said, "Exactly. If you're going to AskJeeves, you're going to Kmart."

And the students get the metaphor?

The kids are so used to my saying things that are totally off the wall. I explain to them that the salespeople in Nordstrom and other big department stores are paid on commission. So it's in their best interest to understand what you want, and be able to help you find and buy what you need—not only in their own departments, but anywhere else in the store! Kmart clerks couldn't care less. They just get paid for the hours they work, no matter what they do. So if you're going to do a free Web search, what you get is what they've got, and you don't know what they have or where they got it. Interestingly enough, these kids know about private shoppers; they're professional shoppers themselves. The point is, you're telling somebody, "This is what I need," and they're saying, "Well, I have these special resources. I have a private sale going on."

It's also interesting to explain to kids—this goes back to the quality of resources issue—the difference between what you'll find in a bookstore and what you'll find in a library, why a bookstore is not a library. For many of them, this is totally new. I point out to them that the bookstore will have only what's current. It will not necessarily have the in-depth stuff you need, the older or out-of-print stuff, nor will the sales clerks necessarily know what you're looking for.

Right. And the bookstore stock may not be tailored to students' specific needs—their reading levels, their interests, their curriculum. The databases that we're talking about *are* tailored for student use. Okay, we know we love databases and we have strategies to convince our students to love them as well. Turning to the open Web, do you have any favorite places for students to go, or tips for students to use as they search?

I tell them that if they're really sure they know what they're looking for, they should use Google, but they should use the advanced search page. I prefer that because it makes them think. It asks them questions about what they're looking for. For instance, it suggests that they consider using AND and OR. A lot of kids, especially in the lower grades, are caught up in using natural language, the AskJeeves mode, and they haven't learned how to toggle off the AskJeeves frames so they can tell where they really are; they're trapped in the frame.

I also send students to LII.org [25] because that will give them a good idea of what might be out there. I send them to the

Internet Public Library [21]. When I do pathfinders, those are the places where I start to find my resources. I talk with them about how I did the pathfinder they're working with, so that they understand my search strategies.

It's not magic; you've put some thought into this, the same thought they might use.

I also recommend keeping multiple browser windows open so it's easier to switch back and forth, and I suggest that kids keep track of where they've been. You should have a piece of paper and a pen next to you; do not assume that the computer will always be able to take you back to where you've been.

That's a good point; so many students cannot remember any details about that most wonderful Web site or how they got there in the first place.

Another point I emphasize, especially if they're searching in school, is to assume the worst at all times. Something will crash and your work will be lost, which is why you always have a backup.

I don't know anybody who's worked in schools who hasn't had a plan B to avoid freaking out. Alice, how do you engage the larger learning community in your effort to improve kids' search skills? You must have had principals who were supportive, or a team of teachers who worked with you.

Teams of teachers. Not necessarily principals. The best way I found was to demonstrate success with a small group of power players. Get a good project with a good teacher, and then let the rest of the building and the powers that be know that it was so successful. I use referent compliments. I always made a point of sending a note to the principal saying, "You really should see this project that so-and-so worked on; it was so fabulous."

How did you learn how to search?

I'm self-taught. I did take one course a number of years ago through Rutgers. It was supposed to be on searching online databases. Unfortunately, it only covered Dialog. But it gave me the background I needed in terms of the structure of databases, and Boolean searching, and the understanding that different databases work in slightly different ways and have slightly different syntax. That understanding carries over to the Web as well.

Alice, what do you see as the main barriers or frustrations in teaching students and teachers to improve their searching skills?

We've already talked about a couple of them. The biggest barrier is attitude: "I already know what I'm doing, and you can't show me anything." The second biggest barrier is the hurry-up mentality. And the third biggest barrier is, "What do you mean I can't print everything?" It's the "gimme" attitude: "I shouldn't have to sit here and read and actually look for specific stuff." Print it out and then highlight the whole page. I want kids to learn how to read critically, rather than just look at a document and say, "that looks long, I'll use it."

What I'm hearing from you is that a good searcher is somebody who reads critically. Would that be your definition?

Yes, critical thinking is essential. A good searcher is somebody who makes a plan in advance, who has a fairly good idea of the best search words to use, who is willing to follow tangents if they look promising, but knows when to stop. A good searcher thinks critically and is willing to dig.

Super Searcher Power Tips

➤ 7 Habits of Effective Web Searchers:

      Plan your search

      Understand Web terminology

      Read the directions

      Select the right tools

      Use Web-browser tricks

      Investigate the authority

      Try alternate routes!

Linda Joseph

Advice from the Cyberbee

Linda Joseph is a library media specialist with Columbus, Ohio, public schools. On her Cyberbee Web site [95, see Appendix] she calls herself "a busy little bumblebee zooming around the Internet scouting out curriculum treasures." The site offers instruction on how to determine quality information, cite resources, and understand copyright and includes a variety of searching activities and Web projects for learners. Joseph maintains close contact with the Library of Congress American Memory Project [83], where she worked for a year on leave from Columbus.

ljoseph@cyberbee.com
www.cyberbee.com

Tell me how you got involved in the whole field of searching, and then how you got involved in *teaching* searching.

Back when the Internet was invented by Al Gore—actually, back in 1992, I got a password and a login to Ohio State University from one of the professors there. I was not a student or affiliated in any way, shape, or form. In turn, I was to report to this professor each week about how I was progressing. This was before the Web, in the days of gopher, telnet, you know—those very early days. It was just trial and error. Eventually I figured out how to do it all on my own; there were no Internet books at the time.

117

That's wonderful. It proves to kids also that adults are as prone to be taken in as kids. Evaluation is a lifelong skill; just because we're not doing research assignments doesn't mean we don't have to be on the lookout for quality and credibility.

Right. We like to start out with an example or two of sites that look like bona fide sites but aren't, and ask, "How would you evaluate this? How would you look at it, take this apart, and determine if the information is correct?" We discuss figuring out where whales live. Could they really live in Lake Michigan? We try to verify the information by using other sites like National Geographic [132] or a marine biology site. You help guide students into looking at reliable places to verify their information.

So evaluation is top on your list of essential skills. What's number two on your list?

Narrowing a topic so that you can find what you need. It's really hard to find targeted information on the Web, even for an adult like myself who's done it a lot. Kids need a great deal of guidance in terms of thinking about keywords. They think they can just go on the Web and find anything, so they just put in whatever, and then they think they've found it all in the first search—on the first page of results *and* on the first try. I work with teachers on looking at a whole host of keywords and ideas and topics, on the fact that you can search by keyword or by natural language, and that they'll bring up different results. Everybody now thinks Google [15] is *it*, and they don't have to look anywhere else. Google's a great tool and I love it and I wouldn't not have it, but you have other places to go as well.

Speaking of other places, when you're working with K–12, what's appropriate developmentally for teaching kids about searching?

The smallest ones probably aren't going to do much searching. I like Yahooligans! [49], although I'm not as happy with it now as I used to be. Of course, there's KidsClick! [23], developed by librarians, which is more of a directory than a search engine; students can get right into specific topics. It takes some of the harder elements in searching out of the mix for the kids. KidsClick! has already looked at the sites and determined that they're reliable, credible. They've helped the kids with the evaluation piece. I am not very impressed with AskJeeves for Kids [5]. It's fairly safe if you want to look at safe sites, but I don't find what I'm looking for with AskJeeves. Often the results don't have anything to do with what I had in my mind.

There's not a lot of competition out there in the kids' search market. There is really no business model for commercial success in this area. What about the pay services?

Some of them are okay, and some of them are quite frankly above the kids' level of understanding. EBSCOhost [53] is the one that I like the most in the subscription arena. I've found that they have been the most consistent in their product and what they deliver to the kids. eLibrary [55] is not bad. On the older end of the spectrum, I like ProQuest [67]; it would be my favorite for high school. You can find all sorts of great stuff in there.

In terms of your encounters with teachers, what are your frustrations? What would you love for teachers to know?

They think all of this means extra time. Their attitude is, "This adds more time to my workload, therefore how do I manage it? How can this become part of my daily routine versus an additional half hour of preparation?"

In your experience, do teachers view librarians as partners?

It depends on where you are—which school district in which part of the country, and the district leadership. It varies enormously from place to place. Where a partnership exists, librarians and teachers do amazing things with students. Students become information seekers who synthesize the material into presentations, experiments, and projects that clearly show their growth in knowledge.

What percentage of the teachers would you label as really competent searchers, or is that all over the board, too?

It's all over the board, but in terms of really excellent searching, not very many people have those skills. The people who do are generally the library media specialists, because it's part of their everyday job.

In addition to having library media specialists around, what's most important for teachers to master in order to work really well with kids?

Conceptually, that technology is not an add-on—that it is a tool, like a pen or a pencil, and that it is actually very effective, and you can just integrate it right into your lessons. If you're going to spend an hour developing your lesson anyway, why not just incorporate the tool into it?

I don't see any problem with having a technology goal at the same time you have a content area goal; having kids do the practice easily gets that goal across as well.

One of the things that's going to help this whole process is to tie the technology goals to the curriculum standard. In our district, we're starting to develop examples of how the technology can be used with each individual standard. It's going to be a monumental task.

Do you see that as a way to really engage the learning community in the effort?

Yes, I do. The standards are required. If librarians show colleagues how to incorporate the technology along with the standards, then teachers will have those activities readily available to use anytime, anywhere, especially if they are put online in a tool such as Blackboard [89]. Teachers and students will have direct access to the instruction. We are using the full Blackboard package to create Web-enhanced lessons for students and graduate-level professional development courses for teachers.

So students are engaged in say, threaded discussions and chats relating to *A Raisin in the Sun* or whatever?

Right. And they can go to Web sites that teach the concepts. We're just starting, but we have a couple of model pieces on now. We started with elementary math. The curriculum guides have been written by the various content professionals. We are tying it into the technology. It's going to be awesome.

Do you feel that the focus on standards and testing is discouraging people from focusing on information literacy? Is it taking attention away from some of the critical thinking skills that we value?

Absolutely. The math curriculum that we're putting up is highly engaging and interactive. It's higher-order conceptual thinking skills. We have some content providers who are actually helping us write lessons, and that's what we're demanding from them. But what is discouraging is that our teachers say, "I've got to do this, this, this, and this because this is in the pacing guide and this is what's on the test and that's what I've got to teach, so how can I do the 'fun stuff'?" Well, the fun stuff can be part of what you teach. That's what we're trying to model with what we're doing on our end in technology—how you can make the learning engaging.

We don't have good data yet because we haven't rolled out the entire package, but we've found that the kids really enjoy the online math manipulatives using Java applets and animation. They also enjoy the problem-solving stories. They're given a story line and they have to solve a problem. For instance, a pyramid is being built, but part of it isn't finished. How are we going to finish it? You can't go and measure it in Egypt. You have to figure out what the dimensions are and how much material you need to finish this pyramid. The kids are given all the different manipulatives and tools they need for looking at proportions. They must determine how to solve this problem.

So those become information literacy problems, too.

Right, because they have to know where to find things, and they're given some Web sites to find information on as well. They have to then solve this problem as a fictional company. This fits right into the standards and grade-level indicators that must be followed. What better way to keep the fun stuff in than to do it this way? It's a big project, but we're seeing that it's going to make a difference. In the next year we will be gathering data to evaluate the project.

You've created some pretty amazing online lessons. What does best practice look like for teachers and librarians who are creating lessons in searching or information literacy instruction?

I look at how well they use critical thinking skills. I've seen some terrific WebQuests [164], inquiry-driven online learning activities, based on the model developed by Bernie Dodge and Tom March [165]. I would call some of those best practice, but I've also seen some pretty dismal ones. There's a really neat one on the concept of primary sources. It's about looking in grandma's trunk and finding 1904 World's Fair memorabilia. The task is to find a ticket, determine which countries were represented at the Fair, and draw samples of postcards. I looked at it and thought, "Wow! What a neat WebQuest for kids!" The site is called Cherished Keepsakes of 1904 [90].

What are you most proud of on your own site?

The work I'm most proud of are the interactive lessons that use all sorts of neat resources. One of my favorites is Revolutionary Viewpoints. It integrates literature and social studies, and is based on the book *April Morning* [144]. We take some images by different artists on what that day looked like from their perspective. Then we take viewpoints of the British leader Pitcairn and one of the Minutemen, based on two eyewitness accounts. We videotaped two actors re-enacting the story of what happened. It's all in QuickTime video on the site. What students are supposed to do is read *April Morning* and then write their own "eyewitness" accounts from the perspective of a farmer, a teacher, a Minuteman, a British officer, that sort of thing. There are all sorts of resources listed. There's also an introduction called Road to Revolution. We put together primary sources and added a narrative to it. We call it our "Ken Burns of the Web." It was a huge effort. We presented it to the Ohio Board of Regents as a model lesson for our state standards.

Another of my favorites is Whodunit [166]; it's about forensic science. Students must engage in all kinds of activities prior to solving an online mystery, The Mystery of the Barefoot Burglar.

Did you invent the whole mystery? That must have taken forever to do.

Not really. You get organized and you just crank it out. Another favorite is the Henry Hikes to Fitchburg and Henry Builds a Cabin activities. Again, my colleague and I contacted the author, D. B. Johnson, before we started on the Henry Hikes project and he allowed us to use his illustrations. We created Web sites on Henry Hikes to Fitchburg [109] and Henry Builds a Cabin [109]. It's a story based on a picture book about Henry David Thoreau, from a passage in *Walden*. You can either take the train or hike. There are different activities to do, depending on which choice you make.

In Henry Builds a Cabin, students are required to do searches and find information about Thoreau. There's an interactive flash module for building a Walden Pond cabin. As you build, you learn about different parts of the cabin and how it is constructed. It's a game, so you can play at different levels, either by yourself or with another team member. It's a really neat little piece.

Then I created Discovering American Memory [99] for the Library of Congress, to familiarize teachers across the country with the American Memory collection at the Library of Congress. I have a link to that on Cyberbee.

Do you use any models for information literacy instruction?

Yes, I like the Big6 model [88, 184]. It is our library curriculum in the Columbus schools. It helps teachers and kids organize in the searching process: What is your task? What do you want to know? Once you know what you want to know, how are you going to find it? You take them through the whole process of information seeking and then using the information and synthesizing it and evaluating it.

Initially, when we talk about the Big6 with teachers, they've never heard of it, it's totally foreign to them. It's different from the lesson plans that they're used to doing. They're puzzled as to how it fits in with their conceptual idea of a lesson plan. Once we get them on the right track and help them understand how to use the Big6, themselves and with their kids, we usually win them over. We've actually had some teachers at the end of our course say, "I'm really glad I was introduced to the Big6, and I'm really going to use it."

Excellent. And you're seeing differences in the way students approach research?

Well, when they take it back to the classroom, we're still fighting the battle of proficiency versus inquiry. Proficiency has basically killed inquiry.

So you're trying to get this Big6 curriculum adopted and it's being killed? Weren't the tests supposed to incorporate critical thinking?

That's not what teachers think the proficiencies are about. They think you tell the kids this stuff and they learn it and then they can put it on the proficiency test. They don't understand that, if you can get them to the point of understanding how to problem solve and think, they can transfer the knowledge. It is very difficult to talk to teachers about transference of knowledge.

But if the kids learn critical thinking in a very engaging way, they're going to remember it. They're not going to remember it if they're reciting it back to you. So we try to get the teachers to think about essential questions: What do you want the kids to know, and how are you going to know that they know it? You do backward design. You start with what kind of assessment you're going to look at, and then you design backward to meet that. It's tough. We have some really good teachers and some of them get it, and some of them just don't.

I'm wondering, in terms of searching, how would Linda Joseph fix the world?

All of my fixes are really practical. First of all, I'd want a tool bar at the top of my page all the time. It can be Google. It's been invaluable to me to have that toolbar right there, front and center, to be able to type a search immediately.

We talked about Google a bit, and we talked about some of the search tools for kids. Do we adults and teachers need other research tools in our toolkit?

Oh, yeah. I would use AltaVista [3], and Dogpile [8] as a metasearch engine. There's also a great tool put out in Florida called SEIR-TEC Internet Search Tool Quick Reference Guide [152]. It's a bird's-eye view of search engines; if I'm looking for this, which search tool would I use? This is one that you can print out to give to your kids. I use it when I'm teaching my course; I take teachers to the SEIR-TEC site and they really like that it's available to them. Students need a search tip sheet to use as they're searching.

Another tip is to remember that you can use advanced search features. It takes a little extra time, but sometimes it's worth it. Also, if you really are looking for a particular phrase, use quotation marks.

What else have we missed about searching that's really important?

When I teach, I have people search on the same term, in different search engines, to compare the results they get. They're often surprised about the differences. And they're really surprised about the number of hits. I'll start them out with something really general and, you know, they get a million hits. Then I show them how to narrow that down with quotes or a Boolean expression, and then they see how that reduces it to something more manageable.

Sometimes when you are searching you find compelling information you didn't expect. I call those "Lucky Finds." Here is an example. I grew up in Xenia, Ohio, and decided to see what might be in the American Memory collections about my hometown. To my amazement I found several articles in both the *Xenia Torchlight* and in the *Cleveland Gazette* about a court case, *McCullom v. Xenia Board of Education*. In 1887, a black girl wanted admission to a white school. Judge Hawes gave a decision in favor of mixed schools but withdrew from the race for re-election "because the sentiment of prejudice was so great." I thought this was fascinating in light of the 50th anniversary of *Brown v. the Board of Education*. Although the McCullom case was not heard by the U.S. Supreme Court, it shows that the issue existed in 1887. "Lucky Finds" like this example can add a bonus to any search.

Super Searcher Power Tips

➤ Preselect sites for younger students.

➤ Keep a copy of Internet Safety Tips [97] next to the computer.

➤ Keep a copy of Copyright Tips [96] next to the computer.

➤ Download a search toolbar such as those offered by Google or Yahoo! to make searching quick.

➤ Keep a search tip sheet, such as SEIR-TEC Internet Search Tool Quick Reference Guide [152], available for students.

➤ Download ieSpell [112], the free spell checker for Internet Explorer, for filling in forms on the Web.

➤ Ask a Librarian [87] at the Library of Congress about their collections.

➤ Search eBay [100] for primary sources such as old postcards of historical sites, hometowns, countries, and famous people.

➤ Use Lake Michigan Whale Watching [122] for teaching Web evaluation.

➤ Download a free ad eliminator such as Spybot [157] to clean up unwanted ad software on your computer.

Frances Jacobson Harris

Thinking About Innards: Why Infrastructure Is Important

Frances Jacobson Harris is librarian at University Laboratory High School and associate professor of library administration at the University of Illinois at Urbana-Champaign. She writes frequently for library and education journals.

francey@uiuc.edu
www.uni.uiuc.edu/library

Frances, what are the biggest issues you see relating to teaching searching skills?

One of my pet peeve topics is getting students to determine the level of specificity or abstraction at which they need to search. Are you searching the full content of the document or page, or are you searching an abstracted piece of it, just the subject headings or bibliographic data? I think of the Internet as full-text land. In the Internet world, items don't have tags associated with them like title, author, subject, as they would in a formal database. Yes, some pages have metatags, but they aren't the same thing. The folks behind the scenes at the search engines, the designers, make judgments about what criteria might rise to the top. You are searching all of the content that has been captured and indexed by the Web crawler. If you're searching a bibliographic database, then you're only searching a representation of the information as a whole.

How do you translate that message to students?

I might start a lesson by asking somebody in the class to take a book out of their backpack, open it to a random page, and read a sentence in the middle of the page. Then I ask, "Would you be able to look up this book by what you just read, by the words in that sentence?" That establishes a mental model about what's accessible. I back up and ask, "What are the other identifiers for the book?" We talk about the title page, the author and the title, and what the book is about, and then we have a little argument: "Well, okay, you say it's about spaghetti, but he says it's about noodles. Which term are you going to use?"

So the kids can see that Web indexing has its flaws, and that's why it's often hard to find the stuff you need.

But if the book were full-text online, you probably could find it. In fact that's what Amazon [1, see Appendix] is offering now. But what else would you find? That presents a chance to talk about a number of other issues. For instance, how much is on the Web and how much is not.

Maybe searching is bigger in concept than we normally consider. What skills do searchers need that might not necessarily be thought of as searching skills?

It's mostly about knowing what you want. You need to have thought about what you are really looking for. We talk about what's an easier search: author, title, or subject—the idea of known-item searching. Internet searching is hardly ever known-item searching, unless you're typing in a URL you know exists.

When you say "known-item searching," you mean trying to find something you know is there? As opposed to a kind of

serendipity: "Here's everything and I have to make a
decision about which of these are the things I need."

> Right, you're looking for a finite thing that you know is out
> there, and it's more of a locational problem. Where is it?

Certainly that type of location-based searching doesn't
require much information literacy. What is the relationship
between searching and information literacy?

> Searching means that you understand your information need.
> You have to have done a little metaprocessing, where you think
> about what you want. You can't be information literate unless
> you know what you want. That's the precursor, the first step. It's
> the foundation. Next, you have to be clear on when you have to
> go back and adjust your search.

Do you feel that young searchers are aware that the process
is recursive? That they might not know that they aren't done,
that the first search might not be good enough?

> Absolutely. One of the things I like about NoodleBib [136] is
> that during the process of creating a citation, it makes you think
> about the information you're using.

That's Debbie Abilock and her son Damon's program for
creating citations. Those prompts for writing citations force
students to look at it and think, okay, what is this thing that
I'm citing?

> Right. Beyond identifying the information to begin with, eval-
> uation constitutes a huge part of the searching process. You have
> to do both simultaneously. You can do an exercise without hav-
> ing a kid sitting in front of a computer. If you are looking at a list
> of hits, which ones would you use first and why? What are the
> clues in each hit that help you decide?

So they'd work from just the URL and the description?

Whatever they'd get from the search engine. What clues are there that would lead you to visit this site? Can they articulate the reasons in small groups? It's a useful exercise.

When did you go to library school? Did you feel that it prepared you for the landscape that you're facing now?

I went to library school in the mid-'70s. What I learned from that experience is that there are structures that underlie all of the searching tools and databases, and what you have to do is figure out what those structures are and how to make them work.

So you see a bigger picture than the end-user would, because you understand the innards of how a database or search engine works.

Right. But you don't have to see it like a librarian. I have never taught the Dewey Decimal System. I've never made kids memorize call numbers. You can ask "where are the dog books?" and the librarian can say "636.7." There's no reason for a kid to stuff his head with extraneous information. What I do think is important to learn is that there is always a tool—a catalog, an index, or a database, maybe a librarian—where you can look up "dog" and get that address, that 636.7.

The tools have changed, though. In terms of retooling, what's been important for you to understand, and to help users understand, as the information landscape evolved?

Let's say the information landscape evolved from the *Reader's Guide to Periodical Literature* [70]. When you move to the online format, it still has the same buttresses, the same infrastructure. It's still based on retrieving bibliographic information. Then you get something like Electric Library, one of the first full-text retrieval products that had no field definitions, no parameters. Once you realize that, you decide you'll have to find another way to limit the search set. You figure out that, if you can't specify that you want the word "snake" in the subject heading, you need to figure out how to retrieve snake the animal and not snakes in the sense of villains. Once you know that, you can accommodate the system by figuring out how to play it. If it's a formal system, like in *Reader's Guide*, then you know there's a controlled vocabulary and fields to search. If it's an informal system, like the Web, you know that you have to impose the structure, with things like quotation marks around a phrase. Interestingly, kids seem to know that. It's easy for them to figure out, and it's easy for them to mimic. It's sort of automatic; they get really good at limiting their search sets. Of course, some systems don't want quotes around a phrase. There are ways system designers can help users.

What can we do to help system designers build a better mousetrap for our kids? What would you like to see designers do as they develop databases? What would Google [15] look like in your perfect world? What would subscription databases look like?

I know how to complain better than I know how to suggest. InfoTrac [59] defaults to a subject search. You type in your term and it takes you directly to that term, but then it also says there are 20,757 hits. And it shows how you can narrow by subdivision.

So kids can browse through the subdivisions for words and concepts they would never have thought to use.

Right. Recognition is a much stronger skill than recall, so they don't have to come up with the term. They don't have to figure it out. On the other hand, it bombs if you put in a word that is not in the subject directory. And then it defaults to a keyword search, looking for the words you enter anywhere in the text, in any field. ProQuest [67] and First Search [66] products don't do it that way. You basically start with a keyword search and look for the magic words.

But they do list the descriptors in their hyperlinks once you get to them.

Yes, but I find that students just want to go straight to those links and not refine the search. So they miss opportunities to use the database's carefully selected subject headings, and they might also miss relevant documents that don't use the keywords the student might have thought were best.

And that's not necessarily prompted as well as it could be. Students really need to know why those little tabs that show types of documents, or those hyperlinked subject headings, are there, and that they can help them refine their search.

Right. What I'll do with kids sometimes is go to InfoTrac first and figure out how the subject might be structured by looking at the subject headings and subheadings. Then, because InfoTrac may not have as much full text, we'll go back to one of the other databases like First Search that has a lot more full text but may not have obvious subject hierarchies for students to examine. It's a bit of a work-around.

How important are subscription databases in your program? What couldn't you live without?

They're very important. The problem is getting kids to use them. We've structured our Web page to really push kids in that direction. You have to make it so they cannot be avoided. They're the "broccoli"—it's good for them! One of the nice things that Walter Minkel of *School Library Journal* [175] has said about our Web site is that we don't put a big Google link on our front page. Students already know how to get to Google.

Walter Minkel selected your site as a Web site of the month.

Right, and he wrote about it in the context of an editorial describing why you should not link to Google on your Web page.

If you were going to link to Google at all, would you lead students to their advanced screen?

I would argue not. I have gripes with Google's advanced search screen. It doesn't really allow the flexibility of Boolean searching that you see in other advanced search engine options. I like to focus on the databases, and the way I make the databases a little sexier is to talk about them as being part of the Invisible Web. I try to show an actual search and demonstrate that you can't find this article or that particular thing through Google, but you can if you use one of the databases.

Can you give me a good example?

I just went through many days of our eighth grade science students working on their cutting-edge science topics. They're trying to find the latest earthquake research or whatever. The teacher and I have already done a pretty good job on what's a refereed journal and how you find research. I pass around copies of *Science News* [178] and we look at how it is organized, the way it divides up science into disciplines and how it has a "what's new" section. This is different from doing a general topic report on earthquakes or tornadoes or whatever. "Cutting-edge" is what makes the difference. So we train them to find out who the researchers are and to find their actual research in peer-reviewed journals.

Can eighth graders read peer-reviewed journals?

That's what the teacher prepares them for. We do a whole unit on the difference between *Science News* and *Science* [177]. The teacher discourages these kids from starting with *Science* mainly because the kids are 12 and 13 years old and it's over their heads. We do have it for our older students. But they can recognize that research cited in *Science News* has been peer-reviewed. In practice, many of them do use it quite a bit once they've gotten grounded in their topics. And many of them get irritated with the teacher for discouraging them!

But back to the Invisible Web lesson. We can take an article from one of the magazines that they would use for their project and say okay, go try to find it with Google. You can't. There are times when it's really inappropriate to use Google.

They might find it by going directly to the publication's own Web site.

There's a chance. But if it's from two years ago, even if you did find it, you probably won't be able to get to the archives. You have to have a paid subscription to the print journal or the online version or both. It is far easier to find these articles in subscription databases. For one thing, you're only searching selected terms that abstractly *represent* the content, rather than the plethora of words that *are* the content in a full-text source.

So, Google is the wrong tool to use because it can't search back issues that are part of the Invisible Web. The Web sites of the journals themselves are the wrong tools to use because the full content is not available. Subscription databases *are* the tools to use because they provide both the access, thanks to their comprehensive indexing, and the content.

Do your students sense that everything's on the free Web?

Particularly the younger ones start with that. I tell them I'll slap their hand if they go straight to Google. We make pathfinders for specific assignments. But the pathfinders are stuffed with databases, too. To me, pathfinders that are primarily direct links to preselected Web sites are, in essence, not really about searching. But that's okay. There are times when you just have to give them some stuff.

Searching is important, but sometimes you just want them to be able to get to the good stuff quickly.

Right. Start here, and you find out what the cutting-edge projects are, who the scientists are, and then you search those leads in the databases.

Don't your pathfinders also subtly give searching advice, like "remember to check the keywords area"?

That's true, and we also list the Library of Congress subject headings they should be looking under. It's a good way to teach searching.

Here's another example. The university this year was commemorating the 50th anniversary of the *Brown v. Board of*

Education decision. A group of our students was researching the event. What do you look under? It's a challenge. We made a pathfinder that listed subject headings and call number areas and pointed to Web sites. It was sort of a mix. As for the call number areas, that's the kind of situation where I see a benefit to having a kid memorize 636, because you do also want to promote browsing and serendipity.

I don't think all students recognize that the book on the shelf next to a book they're looking for might be related to it.

Or that maybe we don't have an entire book on Ruby Bridges, who was only six years old when she integrated an all-white school. But if the pathfinder leads you to a book that discusses the whole situation, and you look in the index under Bridges, Ruby, you'll find what you are looking for. But my other, more cynical, view of pathfinders is that the kids don't read your helpful advice. That's when you work the floor while they're working, and you model. You walk with them to the stacks, you pick up the book, you go to the index and say, "Look, Ruby Bridges, pages 27 to 32."

By any means necessary. Now, I want to change focus a bit and talk about what search tool you cannot live without.

Full text is really important, especially when you live in a small place. I would have a hard time functioning without Wilson Omnifile Full Text Select [73], because it's such a large database and has a significant proportion of full-text content. LexisNexis [64] is something we have access to that most school libraries don't, because we're on this university campus. I have many beefs with them, one of which is the search interface. They have very informal subject tags, but nothing is consistent, so it is totally keyword searching. It just makes me nuts. On the other hand, for projects like that *Brown v. Board*, we also have access to historical newspapers in full text, through ProQuest, which has a much more formal search structure. It's wonderful.

Looking at the free Web now, moving from subscription to free, what are the best search tools for your audience of learners?

Well, Google is the best. I actually don't have any complaint with their basic search. It's the advanced search I have problems with. It needs to have more pull-down menus so that you can mix and match your apples and oranges. There's no flexibility in it. But in terms of the algorithms they use to determine relevancy, they are the best. When I'm with kids, I have them go there first if they're looking for something really specific.

My hunch, though, is that Google's not where you go when you're creating a pathfinder.

Right. We worship the Librarians' Index to the Internet (LII) [25]. We put it on all our pathfinders. I also like the Scout Report [34]. I have a subscription to netTrekker [29]. The kids are accustomed to going to netTrekker and LII; we have links to both on our Web site. With these, the students are not searching the whole Web site, just the bibliographic record.

In one of my exercises, I ask students to find a search that works well in Librarians' Index to the Internet, and explain why it works well. There are two things that I want them to be able to articulate. One is that a good search in Librarians' Index to the Internet is a broad, general search. The other is the quality of the sites that are retrieved. We also talk a whole lot, and this gets back to that infrastructure thing, about who is doing the indexing and that these are people who go out, identify, and evaluate the Web sites, and then index them for the database. netTrekker makes me nuts because, even though they have people doing the selection, and they're supposedly teachers, they've got ThinkQuest [160] sites in there. I think their bar is way too low.

Although people might want ThinkQuest sites for some purposes, student-created sites are not necessarily appropriate as research sites for high school students.

Yeah, I can get those in Google.

You shared a few wonderful lesson ideas. How do you develop your lessons? Are they share-able from your site?

We have a required computer literacy course. I wish we could change the name; it's really about communication and information. They do learn to use the productivity tools in Microsoft Office. They learn operating systems, desktop publishing, HTML, information searching and evaluation, and information ethics. So it's the kind of things you need to know to succeed in school and in life. We stress the ethics, definitely, along with information evaluation. They're kind of tied together. You can get to the course from our Web site and find a lot of those assignments.

I still teach *Reader's Guide* [70], and I still show a video that was made in 1987. The best part of the video is that they show an indexer at H.W. Wilson Company in the Bronx looking through a magazine, scanning an article, and picking the subject headings. Then they show how many magazines are indexed. It's really concrete; you see the actual person, and that they're working with a controlled vocabulary. Then we talk about the Library of Congress, which is kind of the benchmark for indexing, where all the rules emanate from in terms of subject heading assignments for books. You know, why do we have to look up "cookery" instead of "cookbooks"? You can walk into my school and say to a senior "cookery" and they know that the term "cookery" is the word that's going to be used in the catalog. But on the Web, there is no Library of Congress authority, and all the search tools are in competition.

We have made a page that lists the search tools, with a little description of each. It's not nearly as wonderful as Debbie Abilock's "Choose the Best Search for Your Information Need" [92]. But it does suggest, if you have this information need, if you want to know this kind of thing, use this tool. I have students go to that page, and we do demos for different search tools, and then they have to pick one they've never used before and do a search. One I like to demonstrate is WiseNut [42]. You do your search, and then you can see how its crawler attempts to arrange your results into subject categories.

The technology and the search engine products change so quickly, though. It's important for kids to understand that search engine results aren't unsullied guarantors of quality. We talk about sponsored links and about paid-for high-placement links.

You've described working with eighth graders. Are there developmental issues that come into play with regard to what kids are able to do and not able to do in terms of searching?

Definitely. It's that abstraction stuff. Sometimes I think that I should just wait a year, that I am beating my head against a wall.

When you say "abstraction," you mean developing concepts around what they're searching for, trying to anticipate what a search engine's going to do, that sort of thing?

Right, and what topics fit inside other topics. For instance, when the teacher says "earth science," they don't really know what that means. When she says "cutting edge," they're clueless. The way of dealing with that is layering and layering, examples and cases, and modeling, lots of modeling. The teacher will show student papers from the year before, so they see what their work should look like. You go to netTrekker and do a category search instead of a keyword search. You actually demonstrate drilling down through the science hierarchy.

I think that comprehending the difference between a topic search versus a keyword search is a huge thing for kids to understand.

It is powerful. And lots of them do. I just started using NoodleBib, since the eighth graders were doing these projects. I spent a day teaching them how to set up a bibliography. The week before, I'd done the same thing with seniors who were working on a yearlong debate project. The difference between the two groups was like night and day. It was funny. In terms of developmental skills, the younger students are much more literal. You can do all right with, "Here's where you put in the author's name, and when you want to add another author you click the 'add' button." They see the names come up, and then they see when it spits out the citation in the end, how it puts it in the right format. That's okay. But for the part where you're trying to figure out what kind of animal the citation is—is it an article in a magazine, is it an essay in a book, is it an article from a database, what kind of Web source is it?—I think they just need a little background knowledge, a little more experience. It's conceptually different. But, by the end of the year, they can be pretty good at it. And it is very funny to listen to a 13 year old talk about their internal citations.

How comfortable are they asking for guidance in searching?

Very comfortable. I don't know if it's because, for that particular project, they come to the library at least 15 times. We become old friends. They also figure out which grown-up to ask for what. They start asking me what the term "seismic" means and I say, okay, we either have to go to the dictionary to look it up, or you have to go ask Ms. Morris, the science teacher. And when they ask her about how to cite something, or how to find more information, she refers them to me. We can both tell them that they can go to the bathroom. But otherwise there's a lot of referral.

Are you successful in motivating students to care about searching?

If I'm going to be really honest about it, no. It's interesting because, at the beginning of every year, I generally talk to some older students. I say, "I'm going to talk to the eighth graders. What advice should I give them?" And they say things like, "Go back to the green book, keep going back to it, keep going back to it." That blew me away. The green book is the *Reader's Guide*, of course. I thought that was really interesting. So I said to the eighth graders, "This is what the sophomores said to do." And the eighth graders just glazed over.

So you actually have students do a print search, and then go online to find the full text because the print search will help them focus their terms?

Yes, and for two reasons. One is extremely practical; we don't have enough computers. I have five computers in the library. This is a small facility. We only have 300 students. A class comes in with 20 or 25 kids, and there are four or five computers for them. I would probably drop *Reader's Guide* if we had more computers. But for now, instead of queuing up at the computers, they're using *Reader's Guide* to identify search terms. We do have a fair number of the print journals to support *Reader's Guide*. What we don't have in print, we will have in First Search. But we also do other things for expediency, like find an article in a database, print it out, get off the computer, and give someone else a turn. We kill a lot of trees.

What I think that student was really thinking, though, by saying "go back to the green book" was that searching is a recursive process. You have to keep going back and doing it again. Things change. Your search changes, and you realize later what you're missing. If they don't figure that out when they're eighth graders, in hindsight they seem to.

Talk about your teachers. Do they value the skills you try to teach?

This science teacher I mentioned gets it, because she understands the role of information in scientific research, and the role of documenting sources and sharing information and structuring it. She is the first one to say, "I don't understand how this system works; go talk to Ms. Harris about that." She also understands her students' developmental level, that they need to come back to the library; they need to be worked with. You don't just say, "Go find it in the library." She really understands the process; that's a teacher who gets it. The teacher who doesn't get it has a list of topics on 16th-century Europe and tells the students to go and do their term papers on one of those topics. He gives no research guidance at all.

What would stand out in your mind as the one thing for a searcher, student or teacher, to know?

Find the magic "cookery" word. Translate your question into the system's workings.

Understand the syntax and the structure of a database or a search tool; it's not just the word, it's where the word sits. Put yourself in the mind of the database creator. And understand that, if it's the Web, then it's a very different mind, and anything goes. If it's a formal system, you have to figure out the controlled vocabulary they use. Then you have to understand the scope of the information service, like how far back it goes, its depth and breadth of coverage. You find people using the wrong databases all the time; I have had the experience of kids trying to use ERIC, an education database, for earthquake research because earthquakes are something you study in school. It means understanding disciplines, the notion of hierarchical organization. The Library of Congress doesn't use strictly hierarchical organization, but they do use ordered lists. It's like the way I used to think about schooling. You figure out what it is the teacher wants you to know, or how they're going to give the test, and then you morph yourself. When you are searching you ought to be like a lump of clay; you can mold yourself in any direction.

Now let me ask whether there's any one thing that every librarian ought to know.

It's important to know when making students do it themselves is important and when it's not. When does this really need to be a searching exercise, and when does it not? Some systems are just impossible and stupid. One of our issues is our catalog. We have 12,000 books in our library, but it's in the database of the University of Illinois, which has 10 million items. So our items are lost in the search results. And so we browse shelves a lot more than other schools. Librarians should know when to just pull a collection. In a situation like that, you're teaching students to get the information on a finer-grain level. Just decide when it's important, when it's not important, and cut your losses. Not every learning activity needs to focus on searching. Sometimes other skills take precedence.

We met at the Library of Congress American Memory [83] Fellows program. What role do primary sources play in your instruction?

Not enough. But I try to get them in wherever I can. Let me give you the example of a junior U.S. History class. The teacher never lets me in there because he's got this survey course where he has to cover all of U.S. history in nine months. I have always wanted to ask him what teachers do in Europe where they have a lot more history to cover. Anyway, I have always wanted to use American Memory documents with his classes. One day he said, "I'm going to be gone. You can do whatever you want with my students." I thought, this is not the ideal situation, but I'll take it. They were studying the Stamp Act. He and I looked at the Library of Congress Broadside Collection [84] and agreed that it would be a good idea for me to discuss how historians figure out what various points of view were on an issue by examining broadsides from the period. I would tell them about this collection and how you would search it. The next day, when I went to his first class, Hurricane Andrew was raging and the Library of Congress Web site was down. By the time of the second class, I had decided that this was just going to be a lesson about primary sources. Forget about the Stamp Act; I'd talk about how historians use primary sources to look at history.

The Duke University Web site was up, and they had this beautiful collection of advertising, Ad*Access [82]. It's fantastic; it has subject headings, they're ordered, they're hierarchical. They have a "beauty and hygiene" subject heading. So we looked at three decades worth of feminine hygiene product ads. It was really interesting, because it starts in the '30s with this revolutionary new product, sanitary napkins, no more rags. "This will change your life," and there was a lot of medical terminology attached to it. We saw ads featuring doctors, advertising a more flexible life for women. Then in the '40s, the ads showed women playing tennis, being Rosy the Riveter, all because there was an even newer and better invention, the tampon. In the '50s, the ads instead were asking things like "Can you go swimming when you wear tampons?" and "Can single women use tampons?" I asked the class, "what's 'single women' a euphemism for?" And they said: "Virgins!" It ended up being a class discussion about how you could follow women's roles and what women's lives were like through the 20th century, just by looking at these ads.

So the primary sources offered evidence about women's lifestyles, and allowed students to analyze and come to conclusions about the way women lived in the '30s, '40s, and '50s, using information that's not always obvious.

Right. And this was definitely Invisible Web stuff. It's the free Web, but you have to get to the database door or you will not find these amazing resources. To contrast: During the first class, before I found the Duke University site, I was floundering around trying to find another primary source site, and we went to the Smoking Gun [154]. There you can type in Jennifer Lopez and find out what her dressing room requirements are. That bit of information could be found using a general search engine because the Smoking Gun is a visible site. But you can't find the things that are in these specialized collections, like Ad*Access, by using a general search engine because the search results are generated on the fly, dynamically, by the database software. I think I convinced them about the value of databases.

Did you get any feedback from the teacher on that lesson?

The teacher came back the next day and said, "I hear you studied the Stampon Act."

Super Searcher Power Tips

➤ Persist. If the first thing you try doesn't work, try it another way. Don't give up.

➤ Treat each search tool as a puzzle to be worked out. How much of the information universe does it include? Is it a bibliographic tool? Is it full text? Can you use natural language? What are some of its secrets?

➤ Figure out what you already know. Search for information about what you don't know. Read a bit, then figure out what you know *now*. Search for information about what you *still* don't know. Read a bit more. Figure out what you know now. Search for...OK, you get the picture.

➤ Keep your central question in mind as you search. As you look at a new source, ask yourself what it adds and how it fits. Don't be afraid to throw it out!

➤ Try to enjoy the chase. It can be as fun as reaching the finish line. Every once in a while, lose yourself in the search and just wander.

Sue Fox

High School Searching Outside the Library

Sue Fox teaches business and computer science at Hatboro-Horsham High School in Horsham, Pennsylvania. She has taught courses on searching skills to incoming freshmen. Sue also taught at Springfield Township High School, where we worked together to deliver searching skills to students.

sfox@hatboro-horsham.org
www.hatboro-horsham.org/406712583093058/site/default.asp

Sue, how did you get your training in searching?

I am completely self-taught, out of necessity. Information is driving everything. Our students have no idea what we would have had to do at their age. It might have taken days to find something it now takes them five minutes to find. Our ninth graders don't remember not having the Internet in their home. These kids were using the Web when they were in second or third grade. They don't remember not having it as a tool.

When a freshman comes to you, even though he's grown up on this turf, what does he not know that you feel he ought to know?

I find that my students think they know all about searching. They don't. Their parents buy a computer for the family thinking it will be an investment in their child's academic future. But students use this medium to play games and to IM, to send instant messages. When they are seeking information, their friends may give them a couple of good sites, or maybe their teachers give them exact sites to go to. Most students haven't developed strong searching skills by the time they're freshmen. I observe them going to the same search tool all the time. It might be Google [15, see Appendix], it might be AskJeeves [4]. They will type in every single word of a question, and wonder why they can't get results. Even if they offer natural language searching, tools like AskJeeves don't always find the answers. And students don't take the time to understand the format of their query results. Then they become frustrated. They blame the search tool; they blame the computer. They don't know how to use the tools cleverly. Even after you teach them, they continue to revert to bad habits.

So the average student doesn't have a clue as to how to construct a query?

That's right. And even after they're taught, it takes them quite a bit of practice before they truly believe it's worth the effort. A lot of times they can get a decent answer without much thought. But it's not always the best answer. They could always go much deeper and have more solid choices.

Can you actually motivate students to go beyond "good enough"?

Yes. It all has to do with how the teacher presents the problem. We should be asking questions that require students to do things with information—to analyze, to invent, to compare different points of view. The best questions that we as teachers can ask are questions that are complicated, that require the kids to come up with their own theories or solutions to problems.

Searching is really about problem solving and decision making. Students need to analyze a problem. Then they have to go through the process of actually considering their best search-tool choices and how to use them efficiently. When they get information, they have to evaluate it. Is it relevant to my research question or is this just an interesting tidbit? Then they have to synthesize information from their varied sources, pull it all together, and come up with their own solution or their own recommendations.

It's really about critical thinking then.

Oh, absolutely.

You've been teaching this for several years; what barriers do you encounter?

I see several. The first involves our students. They have to experience success with proper searching methods, like using advanced search screens, brainstorming keywords, mining result lists for alternative language, examining the help or tips pages so that they might best exploit a tool's features. Students need to know that they shouldn't necessarily accept the first piece of information they find as the best piece of information they will find. For instance, when students research the Lewis and Clark expedition for my course, they are asked to find information about a man who fell asleep during his night duty. More than one man fell asleep on the job. It's the student's responsibility to understand where we are in the journey in order to determine which of the men we are currently interested in. The student must discern a mental timeline and place the expedition geographically, and will likely have to reject the first few documents she finds. This is critical thinking. The kind of critical mindset required for even this simple task requires guidance and practice. But I am amazed at how much guidance and teacher diligence this requires.

So how can we get students to recognize that the effort they spend on searching will improve their results?

It may not happen in their first searches; it may not happen in their first semester. We have to remind students about good search habits. We have to brainstorm together before we turn them loose. But, after seeing some success, students start to trust that these techniques will work for them and they will become habit, not just more work they're being asked to do.

Another barrier to searching success is the teacher. I am sometimes guilty of this; I think the student has had enough guided practice searching and I assume that they "get it" sooner than they actually do. The result is that suddenly—at least it seems that way to me—they are reverting to old search habits and becoming frustrated.

Another barrier is that adults were never formally trained on using the Internet. They might not know about tools they could access. This is true of both teachers and parents. One way I have found that works, with both adults and kids, to develop trust in the Internet search process is to use a question that they are really interested in. When the search is relevant and there is a passion to the search, the methods take on more importance and the searcher will dig deeper. Relevant topics for high school kids might include researching safe ways to travel to the prom, or developing a budget or expense forecast for the prom event—everything from hair to organizing an after-prom. Kids love to search for cars and learn about insurance, laws, and so on. It takes time to develop questions appropriate for this type of learning. I find that it helps if you have a project of your own—building a backyard play gym, teaching yourself how to knit—and pay attention to what you specifically want to find out and the questions you have when you are learning something new. That really helps you develop better projects for the kids. We can do so much better when we ask for more than cut-and-paste projects.

Can you give me an example of how you might correct poor searching habits?

I can give you one from my own course. I teach subject directories. Even though students have used Yahoo!'s [43] directory, it seems to me that, of all the search tools out there, they're least familiar with the strengths of subject directories. I present basic searches so that they practice using the subject tree and drilling down through categories. We discuss that many of these subject directories are edited by actual people, often experts or librarians.

In effect, they've already kind of edited the Internet. Then we talk about how search engines like Google may find much more, but those results may not be as relevant. I have them compare subject directories, search engines, and metasearch engines using a topic like the Vietnam War. I ask them to go through the first page of results, and determine the percentage of relevant information they get on the Vietnam War with each search tool they use. For a search like this, they can see that the subject directories are much better. On the first page they get really strong hits. But when I ask them *why* this strategy worked best, they can't articulate it. So maybe I should change my approach to "Why might a subject directory be your best starting point for academic research?"

If students knew that the sources they were gathering were going to be assessed, would it make a difference in the way they evaluate search tools?

Yes, absolutely. Asking why a student chose a particular site or resource above others would tell us a lot about how the student was thinking, his or her logic, and the analysis that went into the decision to use a particular resource. This is a really important part of the process.

Do you have trouble motivating some of your students?

Sometimes students who are not really academically motivated just try to get their projects done; they don't see any meaning or importance. For them, we may have to start with projects that really hit their lives, areas where they can see that research has relevance. I teach a lot of 16-year-old kids, especially boys who are heavily interested in cars and fixing them up. Another group is into guitars and music. When they research these interests that *they* consider important and relevant, that's when they start to see research as real.

Do you feel they'll take this new knowledge into the world of work, or even the next social studies class?

Many of them think it just works while they're in school or in that class; it's very hard to get them to transfer skills and ideas from one class to another. That's why I think process skills like these ought to be delivered in a school districtwide initiative where the entire administration and the entire faculty buy into the fact that these skills are important. We do buy in theoretically, but it's hard work to concentrate on making sure the students are practicing the skills. We often focus so heavily on getting through the curriculum that information skills take a back seat. We have so much information to deliver these days; we also have to be extremely creative in our delivery of course content. It is a lot for teachers to concentrate on.

Districts could do more in-service on the topic. Adults, even teachers, may be falsely confident about their own skills. Parents need training, too, if they are to help students through homework.

How do you convince the average teacher that this stuff has value? Especially teachers who may have come out of school recently and feel confident about the Web?

That's a good question. I think it has to be administrator-led. Naturally, teachers are modeling what their own favorite teachers did. It may not be at all relevant for today's learners or today's information landscapes. I don't know how current college professors are, but my experience in taking graduate courses is that they haven't incorporated sophisticated information challenges, or requirements for information fluency, into their own programs.

It would be cool if a librarian was part of every teacher's training.

I agree, but unfortunately, many kids grow up thinking their library is a sleeping place, and in many school cultures it is. Every year when I require my students to get a public library card I am surprised at how few students have them, and how they groan at the assignment. I should plan a field trip to the local library to introduce them to their community resource. I think a library program is key, having a strong library that is an activity hub. I would love to see schools embrace a research culture.

Information fluency becomes a back-burner item, given all the other stresses.

There are a lot of stresses in the classroom. There are academic and learning issues, substance issues, family issues, standardized tests, individual education plans. Teachers are engaged in social work and counseling. Sometimes school is the only safe haven for kids.

So how do you sell this stuff?

It's empowering to know you can find and use quality information, to be confident about that. If teachers have confidence, it's contagious. I've seen that the more success students have, the more they trust you when you tell them that these tools will work for them. It helps a lot if teachers break down the thinking process as they research with children, so that kids can say, "Oh yeah, if I'm not finding it here, I need to go back up to this step and go through it again, and reassess. Have I really thought this through? Am I really looking for the right information, now that I better understand what I am looking for?"

Sue, do you have any horror stories or funny searching stories?

Yes, I have seen kids who base their whole project on a bogus Web site. No kidding. They'll have great presumptions, or they won't go that one step further. They don't trust me when I say you need multiple sources, or to try a couple of different tools. Some just don't believe me. It's even stranger when you know students know better. In my Internet-based course, I teach them a variety of search tools. Their English teacher, who is next door to me, will come over and say, "Oh, my gosh! The same kid who did great research in *your* course will find surface stuff on the Web and use it as a basis for his whole project, in mine." Again, they're not transferring skills. But students do figure out that only certain teachers really assess these skills. Or they learn, after their first bombed project with a particular teacher, that *that's* the teacher for whom they actually have to think back and remember what they learned in my course.

Kids are pretty smart about that. One of the things they learn in school is how to give a specific teacher what he or she needs or wants.

It's not just our students. I recently took a graduate class, and one woman in the last group to present just knocked our socks off. She did all kinds of research; she had a beautiful project. The other teachers in the class were berating her because she could have gotten an A with so much less effort! All of us will choose the low road if we know we can get away with it.

But there are people out there like that woman who are truly learners, who might not have been doing it for the grade. Adult learners often want to get the most out of a course. But you work mostly with freshmen, Sue. Are there developmental issues that you see as you work with kids?

Oh, absolutely, absolutely. By the time students get to high school, they aren't used to problem solving or thinking on their own. That sounds kind of crazy, but it's true. In middle school, most students simply report. My seniors are so different from my freshmen. I ask my entrepreneurship class to write a business proposal in the form of a business plan. It's an intense process we go through together. We start right in at the beginning of the school year, and we finish at the end of the semester with big presentations. They're researching and thinking the entire time. I ask them to interview real people in the community who have businesses related to their proposed business. I ask these seniors to go online and research products they would purchase for their businesses, professional publications in their industry. They're much more apt than my freshmen to go to the library. I tell them that the librarian might know better than I do—and, by the way, after you've talked to her, would you come back and tell me what she said so I can share her advice?

It's much more of a shared experience than it is with freshmen. The seniors see research as a process and investigation. And they see me as a learner along with them, far more than they do in the freshman class where I'm teaching them the tools and trying to give them baby steps so they can go further. I think that's maturational.

Now, what I am teaching may not become real to them until they get that "ah-ha" in another classroom, maybe an English or a science course. That's when the skills become real. Kids often come back to me and say, "Mrs. Fox, I know we did this in your course, but now that I'm doing a project on Shakespeare in my English class, it has meaning to me, because it helped me find documents comparing sonnets…" That's the "ah-ha" moment, when they've found success in other areas of their life and are proud of the result.

Could you just talk a little bit about your favorite search tools?

Google. I love it because it is the best and easiest place to start. If Google doesn't know about my topic, then maybe it is really a weird topic and I need professional help.

How about subscription services? Do they play a role for you?

Because my courses are more commerce-oriented, I actually go to people, to the experts—both the experts in the specific fields and the information experts. Every investigation is a product-based project. Everything is open to inquiry. We simulate the real world; there aren't tests, there's *information*, and you have to get out there and find it. I will often say, "Google is not going to do it; it's time to go to the experts. Let's go down and talk to our librarian. Let's see if she has resources or knows which search tools to use, and let's ask her why." If I worked for a legal firm, I'd have that law librarian. If I worked in a pharmaceutical company,

I'd have the pharmaceutical librarian. In the real world, we have information experts available. I want students to know that.

What you're saying is that knowing how to use the human resources around you, especially the information professionals, is a search skill in itself.

And that kids who are exploring careers, or researching companies, or proposing their own businesses, need to go to the appropriate professionals in the field.

What other search tools are important to you and your students?

I do like the Access Pennsylvania POWER Library [51]. But it depends on the project, the task at hand. I can't say I have a favorite. I don't have them memorized. I have stuff taped to my computer cabinet. We all need to have bookmarks, Web pages with lists of useful sites, or some kind of plaque that helps kids with their search choices, because they won't memorize names and URLs.

My theory has been that you don't have to memorize stuff; nobody does that. You just have to know where to find information and how to use it once you get it. I'm having the best semester I've ever had in these courses, because of this attitude. When the kids know that they're not going to be tested, that they're just going to have to complete authentic projects, they become much better note-takers. They're much more discriminating about what they write down so they'll have it as a resource later. If you don't know the information, and you can look it up on the Internet, go ahead. That's what we real people do. That's what adults do. Knowing how to find and use information empowers us. It is my goal that each of my students becomes a Super Searcher.

Super Searcher Power Tips

➤ Understand what you're really looking for.

➤ Think about where the type of information you need would most likely be: Search engine? Metasearch engine? Subject directory? Invisible Web resources? If you don't know about this stuff, now is the time to learn!

➤ Develop a vocabulary of keywords for your search that you think might bring searching success. Think of more than one word for each concept: college, university, school. Link these words together with the correct Boolean operators, AND or OR. Don't forget to truncate to account for plurals and alternate word endings.

➤ If the first search tool doesn't seem to be working, try another. Don't spend too much time with one tool if you aren't getting results.

➤ Reflect on the process: Are your keywords working for you? Is there another way to combine them? Are you getting too many results? Not enough? Think about how you are using Boolean operators.

➤ Reflect: Are you finding different or additional useful words in the hits that you get besides the keywords that you are using? Try some of these words in your query as you continue your search.

➤ Reflect: Did you really understand what you were looking for when you began your search? You can always redefine your search. Remember, sometimes the answer will be found by putting together information from many different sources.

➤ Verify your findings. Some Web sites are not what they appear to be.

➤ The Internet is becoming incredibly powerful, but you still need the expertise of your local library and librarian for tough information problems.

Ken Haycock

From the Administrator's Perspective

Ken Haycock is a former school principal, school board president, and senior education official in Vancouver, British Columbia. He has been a school librarian and teacher and a president of the American Association of School Librarians. Haycock is the author of *The Authoritative Guide to Kids' Search Engines, Subject Directories, and Portals* [185, see Appendix] and the editor and publisher of *Teacher Librarian* magazine [179].

admin@kenhaycock.com
www.kenhaycock.com

Ken, some of us have to convince administrators of the importance of integrating information skills across the curriculum. Can you offer some wisdom from an administrator's perspective?

I think we have a huge communication gap and librarians don't always bridge it well. I'm not sure that we have really begun to determine what teachers would find most useful to know and use. "Information literacy" is a term that's unknown outside of our field. We tend to use jargon to clarify our own thinking in a complex discipline, but that jargon alienates others from us.

But what we're really talking about in terms of working with teachers is that there are some common elements in every curriculum guide that describe how kids access and use information

161

effectively. Those elements can form cross-curricular unity throughout a building. There are very few opportunities for us to find things that bind us together. So why don't we look at those common elements, try to rationalize them, build a structure that's going to enable kids to be successful users of information, and use that as our cross-curricular context? For many teachers, this approach has new meaning. They can see that it actually can make the world easier to comprehend and easier to manage. I'm not sure that we've always made those connections. We need to help people understand the tools that will make their lives easier.

I wrote the book on search tools because I was quite surprised to hear teachers and school librarians in early intermediate grades saying that they have kids use Google [15]. I asked, "But can they *read* what they get from Google?" "Well, sure," they would say. I tell them Google is an adult search tool. Why do we bother trying to find reading materials at lower levels if the kids are quite capable of comprehending the information they find through Google? Teachers tell me they hadn't really thought of that, and they ask what else is available. Actually, there's a fair bit available. But it's amazing that people are willing to invest time in planning lessons around children's books and other resources, but they aren't willing to invest time in mastering 15 to 20 very good search tools.

I wonder why that is. Many of us are making search tool pages to make it easy for students and teachers to get to those 15 or 20 really fabulous resources. Why is it so hard for us to sell these things?

I think we have to start by selling them to each other, quite frankly. I don't believe that most librarians out there are aware of these resources. I truly do not. I'm not sure how many people, if you actually did a survey, would know about AskJeeves for Kids [5], or Fact Monster [11], or TekMom [35], or Internet Detectives [20]. And if they had heard of them, and you asked what distinguishes those tools, I'm not sure they would be able to tell you.

Is it because their education preceded the Web, and they haven't kept up?

That's part of it. There is also a very foolish debate that still goes on between people who say they favor books over technology and those who favor technology over books, when really they should be focusing on the content, the information, and the ideas that the various resources carry. They should recognize that there's a role for all of them. But when I was president of the school board, I worked with the director of curriculum, and we developed and published guidelines for effective use of information technology and the system. Several of the very simple things that we suggested were never implemented. I was staggered; I just couldn't figure it out. I suggested that we create one graphic user interface for students in grades four to seven, and set it up for the entire district. We would use these search engines and make it clear what they do best, and students would learn to search them effectively.

We do something like that. Our district has a search page for younger students [155]. I'm doing some studies of virtual libraries, and I see some really strong examples of best practice. But I do wonder how prevalent it is. I think that part of the problem is district technology coordinators' control over Web publishing. I know some librarians have thrown their hands up in frustration. There really ought to be a district-level page that addresses age-appropriate search tools.

Absolutely. Studies are showing that what principals particularly value in school librarians is collaboration. Very close behind that, and related to it, is providing informal staff development for colleagues. It's not that difficult, for example, to choose one search engine and have a session at lunchtime or after school for people who are interested. You know, just go through them, one a week. I don't get it why we're not doing that. There's no question the kids are overwhelmed. They *don't* have the abilities that their parents and teachers think they have when it comes to searching.

Do you think that teachers and principals are falsely confident as well?

Oh, absolutely. I think they confuse the kids' self-confidence with competence, and they aren't at all the same. And because teachers and administrators are often poor searchers themselves, they don't understand what the alternatives are. I did a pretty major study a few years ago for a large urban school district. They have 115 schools and declining budgets, and I was asked to spend a year looking at how they could have much better quality library services without spending any more money. So I did all kinds of interviews and studies, and—without boring you with all the details of what we found, much of which was quite shocking, in my view—we made a number of recommendations. One recommendation, which seemed pretty simple and straightforward, was that there should be district site licenses for specific areas of content that is best accessed through licensed subscription databases. It was rejected by the senior director of technology because, of course, "everything was available free on the Web." Why should we pay for it? Can you imagine? Can you imagine someone saying something so stupid in a public meeting?

I've heard it.

Exactly. And you think, my goodness, if that's the level that we're dealing with.... So I responded by saying that there *is* a great deal that's available free, and a great deal of that is not very accurate, a great deal of that is dated. One of the reasons we've traditionally purchased children's magazines for libraries is because they are selected, organized, and at the appropriate readability level. Kids can make use of the information effectively in a planned and structured way. That's what these databases are. Essentially, those children's magazines are available electronically, and it's cheaper to buy them districtwide than for an individual school. I could see that the technology director was kind of perplexed by this, but it wasn't as if her mind was changed, at least not on the spot.

I don't believe that most adults understand this. I do a lot of workshops for nonlibrarians, for teachers and administrators. I ask them to name three databases to which their district subscribes. And there's silence in the room. Nobody knows what I'm talking about. I don't think many of them encounter these resources in preservice education.

That's part of it. Another part is that when we do have licensed databases, we don't make clear that that is what they are. For example, at a Texas Library Association conference not long ago, the huge issue among school librarians was that the state was going to stop funding their databases. What came out of those discussions was the potential impact on teachers. It wasn't that they wouldn't be upset if these resources were lost, but most teachers weren't aware that these databases were actually purchased in the first place. They figured they were just kind of *there*.

Right. And they were cut, and what's happened as a result is a huge equity issue. Schools that can afford to purchase them now do, but there are no state-supported databases for the districts that cannot afford to offer them to students.

And now, across the state, they're paying more than they would have with the state supporting the purchase.

For sure. But let's back up and talk a little about when we should introduce searching skills in schools.

Some people would disagree with this, but when it comes to searching, I don't know why we would start using any kind of search tool before about the fourth grade. For younger children it is best if the teacher and the school librarian bookmark particular tools for kids. In elementary school—as well as in the higher grades, obviously—we should identify two or three search tools and databases that serve the needs of particular kids and teachers in the assignments that are given. Librarians should make sure that teachers are aware of the databases they are purchasing, their costs, how they can be used successfully, and how they can be integrated with classroom instruction.

Ken, what do you think of using information literacy models across districts?

I was quite struck by a recent rereading of the synthesis of research that David Loertscher and Blanche Woolls did on information literacy [189]. There are many off-the-shelf products that schools can buy, but the most important thing is that they agree as a faculty about an information process they're going to use together, and then reinforce each other, whether it's five steps, six steps, seven steps, or whatever. What happens now, typically, is that kids are given time in the instructional day to undertake research, and they're having the greatest difficulty right at the beginning, in terms of defining the task, being very clear about what's expected of them, and understanding the basic vocabulary. They are also struggling with synthesizing information from more than one source, putting it into their own words and into their own context to make meaning from it.

We don't tend to devote a lot of instruction time to these things. As a result, kids don't typically see searching as part of a broader question or problem. They pull the information together in ways that they believe the teacher is requiring. So it's really important that, when we talk about searching, we put it in the context of an information process that begins with students understanding the vocabulary, the requirements, what's expected of them, the essential questions they're asking themselves. I do think that synthesis is a major problem. If more attention was paid to synthesis in elementary and secondary schools, we wouldn't have the problems that we have with plagiarism.

Is synthesis a sticking point, Ken? Even in schools with strong information literacy programs?

Interesting question, Joyce. There are very different ways of approaching a coordinated curriculum around information literacy in a secondary school. But let me share one that's quite relevant to this discussion about synthesis. A secondary school librarian outlined the kinds of skills and strategies that kids needed to complete the typical assignments given in the ninth grade at her school. She met with the department heads to talk about putting together a committee to look at the first year of secondary school, at what they might reasonably do and what level they might expect to have the kids reach by the end of the ninth grade.

So a cross-curricular committee was put together, they identified the critical components, and then they went back to their departments and asked which of these areas a department would be willing to take responsibility for teaching with the school librarian. They developed a grid, and the only glaring hole was around synthesis. Everyone thought it was important, but they all thought somebody else should teach it. It's one of those areas that teachers expect the kids will have learned somewhere else, and when they haven't, their response is likely to be, "Well, they *should* have learned it somewhere else." They should have, but that isn't good enough.

Let's examine some other skills. How about searching specifically?

Students are not always aware of their options. They can do keyword searching, Boolean searching, hierarchical subject heading searching, natural language searching. All of those alternatives are there, depending on the engine that you're using. But they require some expertise. If teachers don't have this expertise around kids' search engines in particular, how can they expect kids to develop it?

And, if students don't sense that their selections are going to be assessed, why should they care about quality resources? Unless you've got some really wonderful self-motivated kids,

evaluation is a real issue. Complicating the issue, our students and teachers come at this at different levels.

Just as you said, you establish the hurdles they have to reach in order to be successful, and then you teach them how to get over them. But you have to set high hurdles. One of the things we don't do very often is preassessment, and then clustering those kids who have difficulty and focusing on them in a concerted way. Why are we still teaching kids how to use the card catalog in the tenth grade? We assume that either everybody knows something or nobody knows it, so therefore we'll do a light refresher. Well, why can't we come up with a simple 10-minute paper-and-pencil test and then cluster the four kids who are having difficulty and work with them, watch them apply what they've learned, and follow them the next time they come in on a different assignment? It makes perfect sense, but we don't do that. And we don't do it with technology. If these things are important, why aren't we doing some preassessments with kids?

It's probably the last thing anybody really *wants* to do, a little quiz on the card catalog.

Or on the search engines they're going to have to use, and that they should have used previously. But when those assessments are done in the classroom, the teacher becomes aware of what's really involved. Yogi Berra once said, "You can observe a lot just by watching." When people think about assessment, they visualize taking a trunkload of papers home to mark on the weekend. But if you divide a class in half, you've got 12 or 15 names, and you're checking to make sure that they can do certain things that you said you're going to teach them, then you can say to three kids, "You know, I never saw you use this particular database when you've been in here. I just want you to demonstrate it to me so I can be sure that you've got it."

Ken, are there any differences between the effectiveness of teacher librarians in the States and in Canada?

I don't think so. It seems to me that we have the same range of levels of support and understanding across the country as occurs in the United States. We have had somewhat better understanding, until recently perhaps, that school librarians must have had experience in the classroom. That was pretty standard across the country with a couple of small areas of exception. We've always understood that *teaching* has really been incorporated into the teacher librarian role. We've tended, in Canada, to have a culture that recognized that collaboration was important, and that flexible scheduling was important. Those kinds of things have been in place but slipped recently because of funding issues. The end result is that we still have people who sort of get it, who are able to explain it and market it to their colleagues, and those schools are focused on students becoming proficient users of information. And then we have other schools where nobody seems to get it. Overall, I don't think that we've developed a very good case for how information skills programs affect student achievement.

You mentioned eliminating jargon as one strategy for achieving this. What are some other barriers?

Some people are simply better communicators. Some people are more motivated to communicate. I've seen some small studies that show that people who speak to their principal on a regular basis tend to have larger budgets. Is this a surprise to anybody? Is it unreasonable to expect that everybody will communicate effectively with their principal? It seems to be an unrealistic expectation for some people. There are huge communication problems, and I think people who have been in the classroom can better understand the classroom teacher's frame of mind and what they're dealing with, and open up possibilities for working together more effectively. That's part of the problem.

In terms of the research, what essential work should we be aware of?

David Loertscher's company, LMC Source [125], which distributes Hi Willow books, published the synthesis of research that's been done in a number of different states. Of course, there's Stephen Krashen's *The Power of Reading* [187], which I understand is being revised. Those kinds of resources help us understand how to develop best practice and how to make sure that others understand that this does make a difference in achievement.

You know, the lack of commitment to helping people understand this and use it is really quite staggering. I give keynote speeches and incorporate the research and suggest the challenges and meanings and what we need to do as a consequence, and nine times out of ten someone will stand up at the end during the question period and say, "Well, are you going out and telling principals this?" *I* can't do it. That's who *you* need to talk to. It's *your* responsibility to speak to the person in your building. I don't even know who they are.

I just don't understand what people are thinking. For example, the work done by Keith Lance, posted on the Library Research Service site [126], is really exemplary.

Right. Lance analyzes the relationships between school library programs and student achievement in Alaska, Florida, Pennsylvania, Texas. It all started in Colorado.

But people seem to think that simply presenting the research is going to result in more money. Well, state and local support for Colorado school libraries hasn't gone up since those studies were done.

The burden of proof is mostly on the individual. At the building level we need to show how the skills we deliver impact student achievement. But I wonder sometimes if I teach too hard. How much do I scaffold? How easy do I make it for my students? How much do I model? At what point do kids begin to take off and really think this stuff through on their own? Vendors tell me search engines and databases

are getting smarter, but I am not convinced. I would like to think I am sending my seniors off to college confident about using the information skills they've acquired.

I gave a speech a couple of years ago on what academic librarians could learn from schools, and talked about what the research said about the K–12 sector, and how that would translate into postsecondary. Well, they're just starting to talk seriously about collaboration with faculty. They're just starting to talk seriously about information literacy as an institutionwide effort.

ACRL [76] has wonderful materials on its site.

Sure, and they were all modeled initially on AASL [75] materials. To some extent, we should make search engines, portals, subject directories, and so on as easy to use as possible. I don't think there's any question about that. But some librarians would simply prefer to work with the materials, the resources, and the equipment, rather than doing the hard work of going out and working with the faculty and the students. They would rather play around with the tools and avoid the teaching and collaborating altogether.

So we should be teaching more actively, integrating skills, creating professional development opportunities?

Yes. We're facing serious issues. In school systems we don't always recognize our interdependencies. Reductions of staff and budget in an elementary school or middle school library are going to have an effect on a person in high school over time.

We don't seem as committed to integrated curriculum as we should be. And we're becoming more committed to standards that are established externally to the school. We don't really establish a well-understood and coordinated curriculum within the building and then make sure that it's bridged with the other schools in our community. I think it's reasonable to expect, working through a district office, that by the end of a certain grade level most kids are going to have mastered certain things, and people are working toward that. But it has to be systemic. It cannot happen in just one project or one unit. When a school librarian has the opportunity to plan a unit with a classroom teacher, they tend to throw everything into the unit they possibly can.

I've got to save these children now!

Exactly, exactly. So they're trying to deal with the whole information process, the dozens of skills connected with that, instead of focusing on the particular skills needed for what they're trying to teach. They seem to fear that there aren't going to be other opportunities. I'm not sure that most people really understand what information literacy is all about, anyway. It's not just about how to use the library.

What do you see down the road?

I would hope that school librarians will focus on helping teachers and students to be effective users of information and ideas. That doesn't mean that we focus exclusively on particular media that we favor, but that we focus on the process of becoming effective users. I would like to see us become more expert in that area than anything else. I would like us to make clear our expertise in working with teaching colleagues to develop a coordinated curriculum in the school, something toward which we're all working. The searching part should be the easiest part of any process. It's the one we pay the most attention to, yet it can be the most logical, sequential, step-by-step to master, far more easily than processes like synthesis or inference.

Another problem I alluded to earlier is that we can't force our language on other people. What we talk about as "information literacy" other people call research and study skills, or the scientific method, or inquiry. People who are really committed and working together tend to use the same language.

These types of changes don't happen overnight.

Well, language can change. But we're talking about changing a whole school's culture. You're not going to do it in two to five weeks.

No, and those folks who approach you at the end of your speeches, asking, "Who's going to tell my principal?", are going to have a hard time making a case. You have to be able to personally sell an information literacy program in a way that addresses what keeps your colleagues awake at night. If you can't sell it personally, I don't think you're going to make a difference.

That's absolutely true. A lot of people are on the treadmill and they don't take the time to step off and think about what they're doing.

And yet reflection is a part of most people's professional practice outside of the library world. Attorneys wonder why they lost a case; doctors wonder why they lose patients; engineers wonder why their buildings fall down. We're not dealing with life and death, but there's no requirement at any point in our practice for us to stop and say, "Hey, are my learners really learning?"

Nor do I think we've put any professional attention into developing highly effective means by which principals can evaluate their school librarians, or really understand what they should be looking for in selecting a school librarian. There's a saying in business that you should hire for attitude and train for aptitude. That's a bit too simple, but we tend to hire for credentials and then try to change attitude, culture, and things like that. It's impossible. We really need people who exhibit personal capability, self-confidence, self-motivation, self-reflection, who are committed to collaboration, who see themselves as part of a team, who are willing to invest in making the team work. But they must have something to contribute as well through their understanding of how kids can be successful in school by accessing and using information effectively, and by understanding the range of resources that are appropriate to a particular group of learners. You need somebody who is a specialist in the resources and how to exploit them for student learning.

We used to talk in ancient times about medium-appropriateness. That's when AV first became important, in the late '60s and early '70s. I think we have to return to that. There are times when it's simply more appropriate to use electronic resources and electronic searching. There are times when it's more appropriate to use a video, and there are times when it's more appropriate to use print. But we have to be careful that we don't box those things in too much, because we know that kids move among media much more easily than their parents and teachers do.

We need to understand that we're working out of a facility that's for the school as a whole, and that our goal is to see that it's used effectively for student learning and performance. It's a complex area that we work in; let's not pretend that it isn't. But the interpersonal relationships are as complex as the kinds of skills and strategies we're trying to develop. I once heard an interesting analogy: We have the facilities, we have the resources, we have the bodies, we have the connectedness with the whole school community, we have the leadership. The question really is, are we going to play checkers or are we going to play chess? The resources are the same. You've got the board, you've got the players. What is it going to be? It's really up to us.

Super Searcher Power Tips

➤ Understand that searching is part of a process that begins with an articulation of the task—the important questions to be asked—all the way through to the means of assessing oneself and how well one has done.

➤ Understand context. The context for the student is not only that overall information process, but what's happening in the classroom as well. In working terms, you tend to perform to your perception of what your supervisor is looking for, and for the student that's the classroom teacher.

➤ Understand deeply half a dozen to a dozen different search engines or databases that can make a difference for teachers and students in your building, and then quietly and effectively develop an informal staff development program.

➤ Understand our area of expertise as librarians, and that our contribution to performance comes through collaboration. If we want to make a difference in student achievement, we need to collaborate with our colleagues and integrate effective searching into a classroom program.

Peter Milbury

How Teacher-Librarians Should Behave

Peter Milbury is the librarian at Chico High School in Chico, CA. He is a longtime computer-based technology user and trainer, and co-founder and moderator of the highly popular LM_NET [124, see Appendix] mailing list for teacher-librarians. Peter's Web site for Chico High School [91] won the first IASL / Concord award for best school library Web site.

pmilbury@cusd.chico.k12.ca.us
dewey.chs.chico.k12.ca.us

Were you searching online before the Internet?

When I was teaching at Chico State and doing graduate work in instructional development and educational technology, back in the early '80s, I became fascinated with the ERIC [56] database. I would go to the librarians at the university and they'd run a search for me in the educational journals. Within a few days I could pick up printouts of the articles at an office in the library.

My guess is you were using the Dialog [52] databases?

Yes, the Dialog databases. As my research focus began to take shape, I started going in a lot, and I'd have the librarians run various searches for me. Then there came a point, maybe 20 years ago, when Dialog became available for use by individuals. I was out of teaching for a couple of years and was doing some consulting in the private sector, not even related to education. You could subscribe to the Dialog databases and use it with a 300-baud modem. It was amazing. At that time it seemed fast. It was so exciting. And I got results, and it did help in the consulting projects.

I was there, Peter! And now ...

Yes! Moving from that to what we have now, it's almost beyond belief that we can find so much information so quickly. Searching used to take up so much of our time. Students would come into the library and spend an awful lot of time trying to lay their hands on information. First they'd have to search a print index, plus any updates to the bound annual volumes. Then they'd have to list all the potential articles, fill out these little slips by hand, and turn them in at the circulation desk. Then we'd bring out the microfiche or the back issues of the magazine. Then they'd have to go over and thread the microfilm. That was so slow, tedious. So much time spent on the mechanics of the search process, the waiting, prior to even getting the articles in hand!

What a lot of time we spent in information logistics.

Online full-text databases have certainly speeded things up. But we still have that wasted time, with our students in particular, and because of teachers who don't know how important it is to teach how to search effectively. But if done correctly, the students can get their hands on the information to make decisions about their reports and projects.

The other things that have been really phenomenal in terms of change are our ability to quickly engage the learner with the data and to organize Web links specifically for particular assignments, units, and lessons, and so forth. It's a godsend. When a class comes in with 35 students, which is our average class size now, they can all be on the same page. Before online full-text databases, we'd often have 35 students trying to access the same books and magazines. Now, we're only limited by the number of computers we cram into our library. We are now able to get students' hands on the right information at the right time. It has facilitated my collaboration with teachers phenomenally. It used to be that teachers would come in and it was embarrassing how little we had for their students.

Are most of your students good searchers?

It is my observation that most students overrate their ability to search effectively. Dr. Samuel Ebersole backs up this observation in an important study on adolescent use of the Web for research [206]. His research confirms that students are supremely overconfident in their ability to search. It's like a tender trap; when students cannot find what they're looking for, they have a machine in front of them that will entertain them. When they are unsuccessful searching, they feel an unconscious need to do something that makes them feel successful. Most students are incredibly successful at entertaining themselves on computers, and also at communicating with their friends, chatting, and e-mailing and so forth. They reach a level of frustration with their searching, or they find a piece of information that is not really appropriate but they think they're done, and then they want to play. They want to entertain themselves. They'll get into visiting entertainment-type sites, chatting with their friends, or sending e-mail. Or they'll browse off to some area that they're more interested in than their assignment. They're wasting all this time.

It is a true challenge to separate students from the environment they live in, a turf that's their own playground, and force them to use it for on-task behavior only.

It's a matter of focusing. That's why I talk about this with teachers when I collaborate with them, even teachers who come to the library regularly. We use these Webliographies or hot lists that I'm constantly creating. I put an enormous amount of time into making little Web pages, lists of links. When I first started out, it was mainly to get teachers interested. I would anticipate what they were going to be doing and I used to lay it out almost like a physical school library. I created my library home page to reflect the subjects that are taught at the school, and organized the links to the pages alphabetically. It is a very simple organizational scheme, intended to be easy for both students and teachers to use. Within each subject area I have created subpages to support both courses and individual assignments, depending on how that particular department uses the library for research and assignments.

Over the years I looked at other librarians' Web pages and refined what I had done. What I have found to be the most successful approach is an organized list of links, sometimes an extensive one. I'd get teachers to look at it and cull it down or expand it. I aim to create a list of links for every class that comes into the library for research.

We make use of a computer projection system to show students how to access these information resources, how to use and work with the information. During my presentations and orientations the students are not at their machines either; they're sitting at tables in a part of the library where they can take notes. Then they move over to the computers and start working. I also create handouts that allow them to get into our databases as well as our Web links from home.

Do you think that students transfer the implicit lesson? Do they understand that you've evaluated and made selections for particular reasons, and that that's the kind of behavior we want them to engage in as they search on their own?

It's so important to have teachers reinforce that the objective for their students is to engage with the material. But when I do demonstrate with our computer projection system, it's amazing how often I have to reaffirm and remind them that this Web page launch pad is a unique set of links that we've created for them, and that they can access it from home. We want to reinforce that concept, and then show them how to get from our top level down into the English section or the social science section or the agriculture section, wherever that specific set of links is for them to launch out from.

You and I work in very similar ways. We both work hard on setting up these links and making them ready for a particular class and a particular unit. Do you worry that you are scaffolding too much, that we really ought to model how we got to those links, and how the students, on their own, can search to find this kind of quality?

Occasionally. But I see so much wasted time out there on the library floor and I understand the frustration. It depends on what the lesson's really about. I do very little actual teaching about searching. I teach about the quality of the databases, how to use them, and then how to use our pathfinders. But I think you're right to be concerned, because they really have to learn to search. One of the things that makes me feel good is that our district has a graduation proficiency, a competency requirement in computer-based information retrieval. In order to graduate, students have to pass a test that shows that they can search and find something. This is very basic, but our school has chosen to have the students complete that requirement in their ninth grade year. They must also take a total of six computer competency tests. Some of the six are optional tests, and one of the options is what we call Web page evaluation. It's what you do with your WebQuest About Evaluating Web Sites [164], where you have them evaluating the quality of Web information sources. At Chico High we approach it from a slightly different angle. They work on Web information evaluation individually. It's incorporated into our ninth grade social science curriculum.

Are the skills that are tested transferred to their everyday work?

I wonder. I hope so. I wish we had some data so we could be sure we were taking the right approach with this testing.

I wonder too. I don't know that we will ever solve this. Shifting gears, now, you and I both value our subscription services. Have you been successful in moving students to using those services habitually?

In the past, it troubled me that the students found it difficult to tell the difference between these wonderful high-quality resources and just an ordinary Web site. Many of them feel that all information is equal. But to me, it's really important to have these good databases. My current favorite is Gale's Opposing Viewpoints [62]. I love the tabs along the top. They allow us to talk about different types of information, and that opens up all kinds of teachable moments. That's where I start talking about quality. If you look across the top of those tabs, where are the Web pages? They're way off to the right. The eye scans from left to right, so they first see the primary resources, magazine articles, and statistical data—the high-quality information—and then they include just a handful of highly selected Web sites. I love the tabs, and I love the fact that they sort them. I always try to point out what is happening with the organization of information into types. I love it. We also have the Gale Discovering [58] collection.

You're gushing, Peter.

Well, I also like what Roth has done with their LitFinder [71].

I think that presents an interesting lesson. Students are shocked that they can find a poem in LitFinder that they couldn't find through a free Web search. The lesson is that Roth licensed the poems themselves, so there's a good reason why you'd find the poem in the database and not outside.

That's right. I often get teachers asking for stuff that is copyrighted, and they can't figure out why it's not on the Web.

In terms of the free Web, Peter, what do you think are the essential search tools? What does your free Web toolkit look like?

I have a link from our main page to Google [15], and I have another page that is a collection of search engines. I tell them that Google's probably, in most respects, the most powerful. I always try to show them the image searching features of Google, or the news. We try some others. I use Yahoo! News [47] extensively with them. I've used Yahoo! Full Coverage [46], but it's the Yahoo! Daily News [44] that I use heavily. I have created an icon for it on the Chico High Library Web page, right next to our library catalog. It leads you to other news sources. Yahoo! is organizing the Internet news for us. You can easily search for news stories, or you can search for news photos. For example, say students wanted a story about Britney Spears. They enter her name; she pops up. And the beautiful thing is, because you're not searching for general Web pages, just the news online, you don't get all the garbage and porn and stuff like that.

Just the hard news about Britney Spears, right?

Right. Here you can search for news photos. For Britney Spears, I narrowed the results down to 43, and although I do see her with a snake and kissing Madonna, there is no porn, and there are quite a few photos with actual news value. There are so many assignments now that require students to use PowerPoint, or asking students to prepare brochures, that they are searching for and documenting images. I spend a lot of time showing students how to find images. Many students tend to go to Ditto [7] first. That is such an annoying place to start searching because of all the advertising. I notice students are often quite surprised and happy when I show them Google's Image Search.

Do you use subject directories at all, like Librarians' Index to the Internet [25]?

Yes! In fact, I'm on their advisory board. I use it personally to find links for my hot lists, Webliographies, the pages that I put together for specific library assignments.

Creating these new types of pathfinders, which we do very often, is a form of collection development. In what other ways do you believe our roles have evolved?

It boils down to this: In the same way that we select books and put them on our shelves in organized ways, we have to be able to organize the Web, the Internet, for specific purposes. I teach courses in the library media teacher services credential program at Chico State, and our students have to be able to create these "Webliography" pages before they leave. I require that my students have an extensive collection of reference sources. They also have to be able to create a Web page that is focused on individual research topics. And I show them various techniques for doing this. These skills are at the heart of that requirement.

If we ignore these new roles, we abdicate our reason for being. It's what we really bring to that research equation. We need to see our Web pages as virtual libraries. I often forget that that's what I'm doing; I'm so focused on it. Of course I also incorporate books and try to work with teachers to get students to use our books. Preservice librarians should be able to be successful at creating Web pages. And they need to start a serious evaluation of what's available out there, both for free and by subscription. This is absolutely essential to their getting credentialed. Every single library school or credential-granting school should be teaching these skills, not only in one class, but in every class where research skills apply. We do teach them in our core courses at Chico State in the school library administration class, in reference class, in the collection development class. Then, in children's and adolescent literature, we have students working with Web resources to stay abreast of what's out there for current awareness. In five out of six core courses, we require that students make Web information pathfinders.

Are you surprised when people outside of Chico High School respond to what you put up, and the guidance your Web site offers?

It's really amazing. From the first year I started doing it, I got positive feedback. It has been a wonderful experience. I hear from the teachers, too! There are teachers who have somehow found our materials through search engines. My pages pop up a lot. It makes me feel good to know that my work is valued outside of Chico High School.

I do a lot of writing on the subject as well. I do a monthly column for our professional association [79] newsletter. I move from subject to subject every month. I've been hearing from librarians that they just copy those columns and give them to teachers; I think that's good.

That brings to mind another idea. Don't you feel that our impact on teachers can be really exciting in terms of modeling selection, pulling bibliographies together, and helping teachers learn? I think we can be even more effective if we can get teachers to the good stuff, and that being able to do this shows teacher librarians in a light that they may not have been seen in before.

Oh, yes. This is what I like to talk about whenever I give lessons to other librarians. Right now there's a phenomenal obsession with research about the importance of librarians and school library services and student achievement. What's really fascinating about the School Library Impact Studies [147] prepared by Keith Curry Lance is the idea of the power of collaboration. Lance notes, quite importantly, the nature of effective collaboration. Collaboration does not occur unless the librarian is perceived as a leader! Leadership has to occur before collaboration happens. The teachers have to perceive us as leaders. Now think of the traditional stereotype of librarians as quiet little mousey-type people, both men and women. Those shy, retiring types who would rather deal with books or technology, who can't get out and engage and teach, who don't want to give workshops and stand up at faculty meetings and promote technology and so forth—those people will not get the opportunities to collaborate with teachers. You're not going to empower achievement without first getting out there and getting yourself perceived as a leader.

And that has to do with two things, I believe—personality and skills.

Absolutely, the two are very important factors. Consider a school librarian who has an offensive personality. That person is doomed, unless he or she can change it. But I've noticed something strange about technology. If you have one little bit of information more than the other person, if you can do one little trick on the computer, they think you're a goddess or a god. It's amazing how these nerdy little kids, when they show some trick on the computer, totally blow away their teachers. Or they criticize the teacher regarding something related to computer use. The teachers defer to these nerdy little guys. They are intimidated by them. I'm sure every teacher has had at least one of these guys—they're generally boys—who just have some little trick that they do. I think that was the big impediment for many years, as teachers were starting to get into technology. Out of self-defense, we have to become experts, as a profession, at using computer technology.

But our skills must be further-reaching than those one-trick nerd types.

Yes, of course. We talk about our students being information literate and technology literate; well, who's going to teach them? We have to be more than information literate. We have to be *proficient*. Since so much information now is brought to us through technology, we *must* be experts. We can't just know how to get into PowerPoint and put up a little slide show. We have to be really good at it. It's the same thing with e-mail. We've got to be able to process e-mail quickly and pull out information that's useful for our teachers. E-mail is a tremendous tool in our reference role, as is searching, of course.

Information and technology are so closely wedded that there's no way we cannot be extremely good at using computers for the kinds of support our teachers require. Teachers must see us as experts in technology in order for us to be able to collaborate and empower achievement.

This may be too dangerous a question, Peter, but how do you view the mainstream of our profession? *Are* they expert? What does best practice look like?

To me, best practice is about continually modeling good behaviors. For example, you have a terminal on your desk. Your desk is out on the floor visible to students and teachers. You are right there, close to the center of the action, where the students are, physically moving back and forth across your library floor. You're as close to them as possible, and on your desk is a terminal. Whenever the students ask you questions, if it's appropriate, you consult it. Otherwise you jump up and lead them to a book or something like that. Or you demonstrate a search to a student or teacher on an individual basis. So you are always modeling effective strategies, you are always in research mode.

Good practice also means having an LCD projector attached to a computer where you can easily demonstrate to your students—not only Web searching, but also how you present the information, incorporate it into your projects, and so forth. We have to be able to do that with such skill that the students feel that we know what we're talking about. We have to be able to demonstrate with PowerPoint, or by inserting images and formatting a document in our word processor, or whatever it is we're required to do. We have to be good at showing them how to use technology effectively, totally integrating good practices into not only their searching but also their presentation. When you look at the Eisenberg/Berkowitz Big6 information literacy model [88, 184], number five is presentation. So we have to do that to be effective. We really need to be able to model and demonstrate these skills and fluidly integrate them into our teaching.

Another aspect of good practice is reflected in how you have your library organized. To me, computers are not in a room attached to the library. They should be integrated totally into the library layout, spread throughout the library so that they're easily accessible, next to books so that they complement the books. My largest group of computers is in a cul-de-sac right next to my reference section. I am constantly reorganizing the library so that all resources are at our users' fingertips. Books, magazines, technology—everything is integrated.

I've heard about California's funding issues.

It's unfortunate at best. Government programs now restrict what I could spend money on, and that eliminated a kind of slush fund that we'd used for buying various things. I think we're the tip of the iceberg out here in California, and I dread seeing other states head in the same direction. I hope it can be turned around.

Let's talk about the future of the field. You're worried about budgets not being supported. Do you see the new generation of librarians having the right skills and the power to turn things around?

I wish I knew. I admire Mike Eisenberg's [101] program at the University of Washington's Information School. I'm sure he's doing well, and Carol Simpson's [153] program at the University of North Texas is also right on the cutting edge. I see Blanche Woolls and David Loertscher's wonderful work at San Jose State [189]. I am impressed with their use of technology, and its importance in each of the programs. I am particularly impressed with their emphasis on school libraries within their overall programs, which seems to be a rarity these days, especially here in California where the state-supported universities have generally abandoned school libraries, and have failed to use their "bully pulpits" to advocate for us. All three of those library programs have very proactive and highly visible leaders who regularly reach out to other educators and the public to explain and promote school libraries.

I can imagine that there are many other programs I don't know about that are doing a great job of preparation. The quality of the students I've seen here in our very, very small program has been impressive. I noticed the same thing when I taught at San Jose State. The quality of discussions on LM_NET continually impresses me. There are many signs that our profession *is* coming to grips with the common problems we face, be it dealing with new or changing technology, or political pressures, or funding challenges. I do feel good about the future of school libraries, because I feel confident in the quality of the people who are drawn to our profession. They seem to have what it takes to do whatever is needed! What more can we ask?

Super Searcher Power Tips

➤ Query your clients, whether student or teacher, until you are certain of their information need.

➤ Get to know the Deep Web with its hidden resources. Keep a list of the best and most appropriate sources, databases, and search engines for various information needs.

➤ Regularly check out new or different search engines and other tools and resources, so that you're familiar with them when they are needed for a particular search project.

➤ Take advantage of specialized search engine features, such as news, images, and mapping.

➤ Make use of phrase searching when appropriate.

➤ Be aware of information quality, and examine your search results aiming to select the highest quality sources. Maximize use of your local- and state-provided subscription services by displaying them prominently on your Web page.

➤ Choose authoritative and primary sources first whenever possible. Explain why to your clients. Primary sources are the closest information sources to the "truth" of what happened. Their proper use in teaching allows students to make informed judgments and decisions, and to develop critical thinking skills that are an important part of information literacy.

➤ Revise and rerun your searches with modified search terms if results and quality are not completely satisfactory the first time around.

➤ Consult with your client after you have given them the information they requested. This may be immediately, or after they have had an opportunity to use the information.

➤ When doing searches for faculty, always stress the collaborative nature of your relationship. This affirms your professional role and reinforces the partnership that empowers student achievement. When searching for students, whether individually or in groups, emphasize your role as an educator; try to connect to the curriculum whenever possible.

➤ For use with classes and large groups, have on hand a computer projection system and make use of it to model and demonstrate effective search tools and practices.

➤ Develop, maintain, and keep current a set of information searching resources as Web browser favorites or bookmarks or on a Web page. This collection is as important a resource as your print reference collection!

Kathy Schrock
Web Guide and Diva

Kathy Schrock is the technology administrator for the Nauset Public Schools on Cape Cod, Massachusetts. Since June 1, 1995, her site, Kathy Schrock's Guide for Educators [148, see Appendix], has been a popular Web destination. Kathy is often asked to speak on issues of technology in schools and information fluency. She is the author of several books, including *Developing Web Pages for Educators* [195] and *Evaluating Internet Web Sites: An Educator's Guide* [196].

kathy@kathyschrock.net
kathyschrock.net

Kathy, you've suggested that we should be moving beyond information literacy toward information fluency.

The fluency idea is not mine; it has come out in the literature, and it does make a lot of sense. We're going from the words "technology integration," which sounds like we're adding something on, to "technology infusion," which means that technology flows throughout the curriculum. "Information literacy" gives people the impression that you learn it and then you're literate and you never have to learn anything else. "Information fluency" allows you to understand that you become fluent in something, but then you can become better. Calling it information fluency makes people understand that, as information sources change, you have to become fluent in the *new* resources as well.

Looking at your students in Massachusetts, where are they on that road to fluency?

They all think they know how to search. They can find information, which is not that hard to do on the Internet, because there's a lot of information available. But the part they're missing is stepping back, before they start to search, to think about what information they're really looking for, and then targeting their searches toward that information need. That's the area that we've been concentrating on, that first, precomputer step.

Does that necessarily happen precomputer, or could it happen interactively while a student is beginning a search?

It depends on the topic. If a student has no knowledge base at all in a topic, we don't encourage them to go to the computer first. We encourage them to look at print resources, identify some keywords, identify some aspects of that topic that they might be interested in. Then we usually send them to the Internet, maybe to a metasearch engine, to get an overview of what might be out there on that topic.

Sending them to a metasearch engine first brings to mind that "Internet as water hose" image. Why would you send them to a metaengine first?

Again, it depends on the topic. Sometimes we want them to get a quick first slice, a scan of what's available. Metasearch engines don't necessarily search thoroughly, but they do give a broad overview. To meet the same purpose, we sometimes send them to a large, multipurpose subject directory, like Yahoo! [43], About.com [2], Librarians' Index to the Internet (LII) [25], or the Open Directory Project [32], and have them drill down through the subject headings to get a cross-section of what's available on their topic. This gives them the chance, before they start their actual work, to go back and refine their question.

I want to step back a bit, because you are a real part of K–12 Internet history. What motivated you in 1995 to put your Guide for Educators online?

I'm a terminally left-brain learner. I'm a technology maven, I guess. I have a huge interest in technology.

Did that start before the Internet? You were messing around with PCs?

Yeah, I'm a library media specialist by training and have been interested in technology ever since I got my first personal computer in 1981, which was kind of early-on for personal computers. So I've been there since the beginning. I was in a small middle school with a very small collection, about 11,000 volumes, when the Internet, pre-Web, first came out. There were all these gopher sites, and I realized the wealth of information I could give to my teachers. When the seventh graders were doing their country reports, I could get the currency exchange rates from the Federal Reserve Bank of Boston. Before that, if someone didn't remember to bring in Wednesday's *Boston Globe*, we didn't have access to that information. I live on a small spit of land in a very rural environment.

So I took the various gopher resources and put them on little card catalog cards in a file box and arranged them by category. If a teacher was looking for something, I could help them find it. Then when the Web came along and we finally got a provider on the Cape that allowed graphical access, he suggested I create a Web page with these resources on it. The idea was mainly to help myself, because I had bookmarks everywhere I went, and to help other educators who were just starting out.

Were you self-trained? I guess there was no training at that point.

Yes, I used the book *Teach Yourself Web Publishing in a Week* [188], and then went to book two, *Teach Yourself More Web Publishing* [188]. There was no one to teach you back then.

So here you are in this remote area, and all of a sudden you're, like, world famous. Is that how it happened?

I think what precipitated it was when, in December of 1995, the National Education Association publication, *NEA Today* [210], found me. I don't know how, but all of a sudden they did this one-page spotlight on teachers using technology. That's when a lot of teachers were just starting, and those people were spreading the word to everyone else. The NEA publication moved things along quite rapidly. My site went from one or two thousand hits a month to 15 or 20 thousand hits a month after the article was published, and then it took off exponentially to a million or a million and a half hits.

How does that change the way you look at your service population?

It's interesting. At the beginning, by finding out how many people were looking at each page of your Web site, you could discover that this area was very well used, but this other area wasn't as well used. That actually allows you, when you are creating a directory, to move things around where people will most likely find them. It helped me develop my Web pages by seeing where people went. Now, I get so much e-mail from educators that I have a good feel for what teachers need and want, and, of course, I'm still working in the schools. I get a good feel from across the U.S. for what the trends are, which is very helpful when adding sites to the list.

Way back when I was in library school, we looked at collection usage patterns offline very much the same way, for collection development and to better meet users' needs. The metaphor extends easily to the online environment.

Yes, exactly. But in library school—precomputer of course—we were told that, if you purchased something that was biased on one side, you had to purchase something that was biased on the other side in order to balance the collection, rather than just running down the moral middle of the road.

I often say at conferences that I went to library school before personal computers and we had 15 minutes of online ERIC search time through Dialog. We dialed up using an acoustic coupler, and all we obtained was an abstract, not the full text. I was so excited about *any* information at that point.

In library school we learned to conduct a reference interview, where you would ask me a question that was very broad, and I, as the library media specialist in training, would ask you questions back. I had to try to elicit from you the question or the information you were really looking for before I could actually help. I often say we need everyone in the world to behave just like library media specialists, to know how to conduct a reference interview with *themselves* to narrow down the information they need, then how to search for it effectively, and then how to evaluate if what they find is any good. We need everyone to look and feel just like library media specialists.

Is that the way you teach evaluation—through understanding bias and selection as people select materials for their own research? I imagine the skills you value, teaching both the public and your student population, are very similar to what we see in *Information Power* [186], the national standards for school libraries.

Yes, no question about it. Figuring out your information needs and figuring out the resource that would best meet your information needs are big ones. The free Internet and the free Web are so prevalent in schools that students often overlook the subscription databases and the wonderful print reference collections that are right there at their fingertips.

What strategies do you have to get kids to go back to, or to focus on, those?

With the younger students I used to challenge them to find something. For instance, I challenged them to find a crop map of

West Virginia. They would spend an awful lot of time on the Internet searching for a map that would show what crops were grown in which part of West Virginia. By the time they turned around, I'd have 15 atlases out on the tables with all the information they needed and much more. This led them to realize that a better use of their time would be to think, first, "Where's the best place I could find the information?" They have to be educated, of course, about what that best place would be. Once they are, it's a life skill. I convinced them of that, no question.

Your kids were wonderful and they said, "Oh, Mrs. Schrock, I believe you now." But do you find that some kids don't believe you, despite the evidence?

The barriers come when I can't provide the information in the school setting. I might not have the resource. Then they point out to me very quickly, "Look how fast I found it online." And then I have to say, "Well, let's look at this critically. Who wrote this? When did they do it? Where are they from? What is their background relative to this information they're putting out?" I don't tell them that the Internet is the last place to look; it's not always the last place to look. But they need to understand that, once they find information, the next part is how to figure out if it meets their needs, and then, if it's any good at all.

One of the things I'm discovering, though, is that what I value, and what I ask kids to value, may not be obviously valuable unless students sense that their teachers value it, too. Have you been successful with that? Are your teachers already there when they come in with their classes?

I think that teachers everywhere can always be reminded about their mentoring role. If, when they're looking for information in support of instruction, they demonstrate that they are respecting copyright and fair use, and if they use reference books and not just printouts from the Internet, the students will quickly understand that, although their teachers are techno-savvy, they didn't turn to the Internet first because they knew a better source for the information.

I don't work so much with kids anymore, I work with the teachers. And the things that I'm really pushing with our teachers are the copyright and fair use issues. I talk about this a lot and it makes teachers uncomfortable. They need to always stick to the rules, regulations, and recommended guidelines if we are to raise a population of students who care about intellectual property rights. It doesn't make me unpopular, but when I talk about it, people avoid looking me in the eye and then there are invariably questions at the end: "Do you mean we can't do this? Do you mean we can't do that?" I always say, "I'm not a copyright lawyer, but here are the guidelines."

What are some of the most common copyright or fair use misconceptions?

The one that's most abused, unintentionally, is use of images—not necessarily clip art, but pictures they pick up from something like Google's [15] image search. Sometimes they just grab images and stick them wherever they want. Even though it states "this may be copyrighted, do not use without permission," they feel that, if it's on the free Internet, they're allowed to use it.

Google's frames often obscure the original source of the image, and that becomes a little dangerous.

Right, and it's hard to get permission. But there are enough images out there that you could easily use a different one.

You speak to groups of librarians and teachers. In terms of teaching search skills, what does best practice look like to you?

For searching skills, I think that Joyce Valenza's original *Power Tools* [204], Volume 1, works very well, although *Power Research Tools* [203] and *Power Tools Recharged* [205] are good, too. I love the forms. In order to learn how to search effectively, you have to have a written-down plan the first few hundred times you do a search. After that, it should be built into your research process; you shouldn't have to write it down. It's like the way you practiced your multiplication tables until you knew how to do them without thinking about them. The same with evaluation. Having some kind of graphic organizer in front of you helps people who can't see the big picture. For people who *can* see the big picture, it allows them to look at the steps. So having a graphic organizer, and going through it as a process, represents best practice for me.

I add sites to the Guide for Educators every day. I go through 27 criteria in my mind as I'm looking at a site. I think everyone needs to have something in their mind. Think about the site that would most probably have the specific words that you want on your ideal site. What would it look like, what would it feel like? Then look specifically for that type of information, rather than aimlessly wandering.

People outside of the information world don't realize what metacognitive skill searching is. When I'm searching, I'm trying to see things in columns and rows. There's a plan B in case the first try doesn't work. I'm right-brained, but my organizer is there in all its messiness. Have you seen anything that effectively transmits the idea of this big picture to kids? What works for you in helping kids get their arms around something this big?

One thing that's helped is paying real attention to national and state standards, and to the essential questions. Which are essential questions at the unit level? As teachers get more practice creating essential questions for their units, they become much better at helping students come up with essential questions for their research. It becomes second nature for them: "Well, that's too large. There isn't enough to explore there. Let's underline the significant words. Let's come up with some synonyms." Things like that.

Developmentally, at what point do we teach what?

We don't have students do open searching on the Web before grade six. Teachers are provisioning or preselecting sites and leading students to the information that they want them to use. In elementary school, they're reading for meaning. They're reading to get a knowledge base in a topic. We put the organizers in place in sixth grade with a slightly modified citation scheme. By grade seven they're doing full MLA-style documentation. We have modified MLA for younger kids just so they start to understand about intellectual property from grade one on. This way, children learn the Fair Use Guidelines [102] and to cite anything they use that falls within those guidelines. If the amount or type of use falls outside of the Guidelines, they need to ask permission of the creator and still cite.

From grade seven to grade twelve, what happens? What's important and when do you introduce it?

Critical evaluation is key at this point. We use bogus sites with students. It's very interesting how literal seventh graders are. Sometimes they don't believe it even after you tell them that a site is fake.

I had the same experience. We developed an evaluation WebQuest [164] for eighth graders with several clinkers. They actually favored the bogus sites.

Right, exactly. We had students do entire reports in small groups on the dangers of dihydrogen monoxide. I sent them to the Web site [98] by Don Descy at Mankato State University, which talks about this colorless, odorless substance, which can burn you and can also freeze your fingers and so forth. Of course, dihydrogen monoxide is water, H_2O. They worked in groups and did PowerPoint presentations on dihydrogen monoxide and what we can do to keep the world safe from it. And when they're done, when you tell them that it's water, they look at you aghast. Then they read it again, and they laugh. It's a very fun page. It's probably the one site that can be used with the younger—say, seventh grade—students. Some of the other bogus sites you have to be a little bit careful of; some require a substantial knowledge of the topic.

So we start the citations as early as possible. The search skills we start by having all the bookmarks set to the advanced pages of the search engines. They never start on the front page of Google, but always on the advanced search page.

My students were a little angry when I did that to them. But I told them it was like oatmeal and vitamins; it was really good for them.

There was never any other way in our district! On the advanced screens they really can see how they're creating and limiting their searches, which is very important for students. Once they find out you can limit your results to PowerPoint presentations, for instance, they're very excited. So we do that. We teach searching in seventh and eighth grades, and in sixth grade just a little. For sixth grade, we usually stick to the large multipurpose directories like Yahooligans! [49], HomeworkSpot.com [18], and the Multnomah County Library Homework Center page [28].

What do you teach teachers about searching? Do you bring in the new teachers or do you do ongoing workshops?

We do ongoing professional development workshops. Sometimes it's 10 or 15 minutes at a faculty meeting where we'll show teachers a new search engine. But teachers—actually, people in general—don't like a lot of change. So we've chosen Google as our primary search tool, and we start with the advanced search page or show them things that impact them personally, like Froogle [14], or some of the other Google subsites like Google News, which is very helpful for them if they're trying to catch up on a current event and get all sides of the story right away. We try to teach them little bits and pieces about this one search tool, and then explain, "Here are some other ones, and on our Web page we provide links to those." And we encourage them strongly to read the help files so they know what the search engine or directory is trying to do for them.

Is motivating students and teachers to care about searching skills a no-problem kind of thing?

We have parents come for open house, and they'll say, "I can't believe what my son and/or daughter came home and taught me about searching." So we know that these skills are actually being used at home, which is great. They're very excited. They're like, "Wow, you can do that?" In our state, by the end of eighth grade, these skills are all supposed to be ingrained. That's a state standard. In our new Massachusetts Recommended PreK–12 Instructional Technology Standards [128], we have to show that students are competent in basic computer operations and searching and evaluation by the end of eighth grade. I don't quite know how we're going to demonstrate that, but I have until 2007 to figure it out. I'm hoping it's going to be a practical test, where a student will be given a choice of a subject area, a choice of a topic within that subject area, and then asked to go do what they have to do, based on something they're interested in. That's what I would like to see.

So, Google is the search engine of choice in your district. But do you have any favorite less-traditional tools that you suggest to teachers and students?

I talk a lot about KartOO [22], a visual search engine that shows you graphically where your search appears, based on the database of sites that it has collected. WebBrain [40] is another one that does the same thing, except WebBrain displays the visual search above and textual search below on the same screen. If you use it enough, you might get a feel for how the Internet is organized, and what types of information are out there and what types are totally missing. You might get a graphical display that is not very "busy" on a topic, which would lead you to believe that there isn't much information available. But you can't always make those assumptions, because you don't know how they're collecting data and you don't know how big their site index actually is. But I think the visual search engine is the way things are going to go. I'm not real happy with that because I don't work well in that environment; I'm more textual.

I don't think those mind maps that are created on the fly are always all that logical. I know they're designed to show interconnectedness. I find it very intriguing and pretty, but I don't always see the relationships.

They had to program their spider to collect in a certain way, and I always have to wonder, were they information specialists? I don't know. Few kids understand the popularity aspect of Google; when more people link to a site, that makes it more relevant. I worry about the role good public relations plays in placement on the search results list. Google's not working strictly on popularity these days, but it seems too big in their relevancy formula. If more people link to you, your site is ranked as more relevant than a site that might be identical to yours in all other aspects.

So why don't we teach kids to evaluate how links get their relevance on Google?

Exactly, and have them conduct a backward search in Google to find out who links to those sites. All they have to do is type in link: followed by the URL in question. Have them see that there's you, who is linking for educational purposes, and then there are all these other sites that may not be linking for the same reason. Students need to know that linking raises the relevancy of a site, but a highly ranked site is not necessarily the most relevant site for them.

Most folks don't really think about how a search engine determines relevance.

When the Web first came out, I wrote to the people that make the decisions on rules for the Internet, the W3 Consortium [162], and asked if they could possibly use either the Sears subject headings [151] or the LC subject headings [123]. Those systems were already out there and used all over the world to categorize information. They wrote back and said they didn't think so; they could not impose that on anyone. But, what would have happened if someone more influential than me had taken up the cause and, somehow, succeeded. It would have made things a lot easier. The whole search world would be transformed!

Kathy, if you had been successful in this endeavor, you might have destroyed a whole lot of free enterprise, or at least nipped it in the bud.

Probably. Where would Google be? Where would AltaVista [3] be? Rather than trying to figure out if a word is spelled C-O-L-O-R or C-O-L-O-U-R, depending on the country, a student could go to a thesaurus, use a controlled vocabulary. Imagine!

It would be an infotopia!

Kathy Schrock's infotopia.

I love it. Let's make one of those.

I think it's too late.

Do you have any strategies for motivating students to care more about searching and the results they're getting?

It's a time-factor thing. If we wheel a computer into the classroom for 42 minutes, they're motivated to find as much as they can find in those 42 minutes. On Cape Cod it's very hard to get a feel for the "digital divide" thing, because kids don't like to admit if they don't have computers at home. We do still have a lot of dial-up access, I know that, which means that a lot of the new and exciting things that take a bigger bandwidth are not accessible to some of our students. So they're gathering as much information as they can in the classroom, because they can't do it at home, they can't get it to work, they can't get to the library, and so on. Are they looking for the best information that's out there? I'm hoping that they're going through the stuff they find and picking out the best, but I don't think that's always true.

Any last thoughts about searching in the K–12 environment?

The most important thing about searching is to remember not to start your information process with a search. Start with a question or an information need clearly defined, so you know when you've found what you want. You can always broaden the search later. You don't want to make it so specific that you only find one page of information, because then there's nothing to compare it to. Make sure you have a knowledge base on the topic; look through some print sources to get a bit of background knowledge before you start the search. Don't forget about the subscription databases, which our library system in this state gives to us; that's a wonderful thing. Use whichever service is best for the age level of the student.

I'm thinking of replicating a version of Debbie Abilock's Choose the Best Search for Your Information Need [92]. We're going to do that for the subscription services that we have available for free. When students are at home, they'll have that information and they'll know which one to turn to. This should eliminate a lot of their frustration at not finding what they're looking for.

Excellent idea. You'll help all of Massachusetts and probably become world famous for yet another amazing Kathy Schrock guide!

Super Searcher Power Tips

➤ Learn how to use one large search engine well. Practice with it and read the help files and FAQs.

➤ Do try other large search engines, too. They all have different gathering techniques, and you might find some new information.

➤ Become familiar with various subject portals created by experts in the field you are researching.

➤ Learn about the Invisible Web and how to "find" it.

➤ Before starting any search, try to pin down your quest in terms of a really good reference question that will guide you as you navigate the Internet.

➤ Before starting any search, visualize the page that you would ideally like to find. This will help you recognize it when you find it.

➤ Learn how to do a "backward search" from a Web page that you feel meets your needs. You will often find other sites that are helpful, too.

➤ While trying to come up with your information strategies, start with a metasearch engine or a large, multi-subject directory to get a "snapshot" of what may be out there.

➤ Use a graphic organizer for your searches until you have internalized the process of defining your reference need, coming up with keywords and synonyms, and identifying the sources you are going to use.

➤ Remember—content is king. Navigability is helpful, too, but finding credible, authoritative information that meets your information need is what it is all about.

Appendix:
Referenced Sites and Sources
www.infotoday.com/supersearchers

SEARCH TOOLS (FREE WEB)

1. **A9**
   a9.com/
   Combines results from Google, Amazon's Search Inside the Book, reference results from GuruNet, movies results from IMDB, and more in a multiple column interface.

2. **About.com**
   about.com/
   Subject-based search tool featuring nearly 500 expert human guides, who create original content and gather links in their areas of specialty.

3. **AltaVista**
   www.altavista.com/
   One of the leading general purpose search engines, featuring the Babel Fish translation service.

4. **AskJeeves**
   ask.com/
   Natural language and question-answering search tool now incorporating Teoma's search technology.

5. **AskJeeves for Kids**
    www.ajkids.com/
    Children's natural language and question-answering search tool.
    When Jeeves doesn't know the answer, it metasearches selected
    age-appropriate tools.

6. **Bloglines**
    www.bloglines.com/
    Comprehensive tool for searching, publishing, and sharing news
    feeds, blogs, and Web content.

7. **Ditto**
    ditto.com/
    Visual search engine that displays thumbnail results.

8. **Dogpile**
    dogpile.com/
    Popular metasearch engine.

9. **Eurekster**
    eurekster.com/
    Search engine featuring personalized results determined by human
    networks, what "you and like-minded people think."

10. **Excite**
    excite.com/
    Popular portal and longtime general purpose search engine.

11. **Fact Monster**
    www.factmonster.com/
    Reference resource for children featuring content from Information
    Please.

12. **FindLaw**
    www.findlaw.com/
    Well-respected search tool for legal resources.

13. **Friendster**
    www.friendster.com/
    Popular online community and friend-finding tool based on interest profiles.

14. **Froogle**
    froogle.google.com/
    Google's product search service.

15. **Google**
    www.google.com/
    Vastly popular search engine that incorporates link popularity in determining relevance.

16. **Google Labs**
    labs.google.com/
    Google's beta test area for emerging search ideas and enhancements.

17. **Groxis (Grokker)**
    www.groxis.com/service/grok
    Search engine that visually maps results into subject categories.

18. **HomeworkSpot**
    homeworkspot.com/
    Part of the StartSpot Network, a portal with rich student resources.

19. **HotBot**
    www.hotbot.com/
    Popular longtime general purpose search engine with extensive advanced search features.

20. **Internet Detectives**
    www.madison.k12.wi.us/tnl/detectives/
    Madison (WI) Metropolitan School District's student-generated library of curriculum-relevant Web sites.

21. **Internet Public Library**
    www.ipl.org/
    The first public library "by and for the Internet community" features a wealth of original content, pathfinders, reference tools, space for kids and teens, and much more.

22. **KartOO**
    kartoo.com/
    Multilanguage metasearch engine that displays results visually in maps, showing interconnections among keywords.

23. **KidsClick!**
    kidsclick.org/
    Highly selective subject directory for elementary and middle school students, designed and maintained by librarians.

24. **KillerInfo**
    killerinfo.com/
    Metasearch engine that searches the Web and its proprietary databases and clusters results in Search Results Guides.

25. **Librarians' Index to the Internet**
    lii.org/
    A searchable, annotated subject directory with quality sites selected and evaluated by librarians. LII's motto is "information you can trust."

26. **Meetup**
    www.meetup.com/
    Connects people in Meetup Groups to share causes or interests and meet regularly face-to-face.

27. **Mooter**
    www.mooter.com/
    Search engine that clusters results by category.

28. **Multnomah County Library Homework Center**
www.multcolib.org/homework/index.html
Portland, Oregon–area public library's collection of pathfinders designed around curricular needs.

29. **netTrekker**
www.nettrekker.com/
Subscription-based search engine designed for school use.

30. **Northern Light**
northernlight.com/
Business-oriented search engine that pioneered clustering of results and offered both free and fee-based Web resources.

31. **One Look**
onelook.com/
Offers an aggregated search through online dictionaries.

32. **Open Directory Project**
dmoz.org/
Largest human-edited subject directory on the Web, constructed and maintained by a global community of volunteer editors.

33. **Scirus**
www.scirus.com/
Search tool for science-specific searching; includes both free and proprietary content.

34. **Scout Report**
scout.wisc.edu/Reports/ScoutReport/Current/
Weekly news about Internet resources selected, researched, and annotated by professional librarians and subject matter experts.

35. **TekMom**
www.tekmom.com/search/
Mother-maintained subject directory and collection of children's search tools.

36. **Teoma**

    teoma.com/

    A general purpose search engine, now owned by AskJeeves, that includes a Refine feature and a Resources section of sites selected by experts and enthusiasts.

37. **Topix**

    www.topix.net/

    Comprehensive news portal featuring news from more than 7,000 sources.

38. **Visual Thesaurus**

    www.visualthesaurus.com/online/index.jsp

    Subscription reference tool that creates interactive maps around word meanings.

39. **Vivisimo**

    vivisimo.com/

    Innovative clustering search engine.

40. **WebBrain**

    www.webbrain.com/html/default_win.html

    Visual search engine that generates a dynamic image of results.

41. **WebFeat**

    www.webfeat.org/

    Federated search product that leads users to library catalogs and databases as well as the free Web.

42. **WiseNut**

    wisenut.com/

    General search engine that creates subject categories on the fly in its WiseGuides.

43. **Yahoo!**

    www.yahoo.com/

    Leading general interest search engine, subject directory, and portal.

44. **Yahoo! Daily News**
   dailynews.yahoo.com/
   Customized and personalized news pages, as well as e-mail alerts.

45. **Yahoo! Directory**
   dir.yahoo.com/
   One of the Web's first comprehensive general subject directories.

46. **Yahoo! Full Coverage**
   story.news.yahoo.com/fc?tmpl=fc&cid=34&in=top
   Impressive indexing of top news stories from various sources in all areas.

47. **Yahoo! News**
   news.yahoo.com/
   Comprehensive collection of news from a variety of sources.

48. **Yahoo! News RSS**
   news.yahoo.com/rss
   Yahoo!'s free RSS newsfeed service.

49. **Yahooligans!**
   yahooligans.yahoo.com/
   Yahoo!'s popular subject directory for children.

SUBSCRIPTION SERVICES

50. **ABC-CLIO**
   www.abc-clio.com/
   Individual social science databases—American History, American Geography, World History, World Geography, American Government, State Geography—with strong curricular relevance.

51. **Access Pennsylvania POWER Library**
   www.powerlibrary.org/Interface/POWER.asp?id=pl3441
   A collection of full-text databases offered as a service of

Pennsylvania's public libraries, school libraries, and the Pennsylvania State Library.

52. **Dialog**
www.dialog.com/
Pioneering fee-based online information retrieval service offers a collection of 600 specialized databases.

53. **EBSCOhost**
www.epnet.com/school/default.asp
A rich suite of reference and periodical databases for K–12 users.

54. **EBSCO Magazine Article Summaries**
www.epnet.com/TitleLists/html/mq_h1.htm
Indexing, abstracting, and full text from general and special interest magazines and some newspapers.

55. **eLibrary**
www.proquestk12.com/
Full-text comprehensive database offering periodicals, images, radio and television transcripts, reference, audio-visual material, and more.

56. **ERIC**
www.eric.ed.gov/
The Education Resources Information Center (ERIC), sponsored by the Institute of Education Sciences (IES) of the U.S. Department of Education, offers an archive of journal and nonjournal education literature.

57. **Facts On File News Services**
www.facts.com/
Full-text database of news, charts, images, and more, dating back to October 1940.

58. **Gale Discovering Series**
www.gale.com/DiscoveringCollection/

Full-text databases with strong curricular content designed for middle and high school students in the areas of literature, history, biographies, science, and social studies.

59. **Gale InfoTrac Custom Newspapers, Custom Journals**
    www.gale.com/CustomNews/
    www.gale.com/pdf/facts/CustomJournals.pdf
    Gale's custom collections of newspapers and journals allow libraries to select content to meet users' needs.

60. **Gale Kids InfoBits**
    www.gale.com/pdf/facts/kidsInfo.pdf
    Elementary reference and periodical content presented in a highly visual format.

61. **Gale Literature Resource Center**
    www.gale.com/LitRC/
    Impressive source of full-text literary criticism and author biography.

62. **Gale Opposing Viewpoints**
    www.galegroup.com/pdf/facts/ovrc.pdf
    Outstanding source of full-text material for hot issues research, the database includes viewpoint essays, journal articles, newspapers, primary sources, statistics, and selected Web sites.

63. **Gale Science Resource Center**
    infotrac.galegroup.com/galenet/science_trl
    An in-depth, curriculum-oriented science database aimed at high school users.

64. **LexisNexis**
    www.lexisnexis.com/
    Major provider of online legal information (Lexis) and specialized databases for other professions, education, and general news and information (Nexis).

65. **netLibrary**
   www.netlibrary.com/
   A major database source of full-text e-book content.

66. **OCLC First Search**
   www.oclc.org/firstsearch/default.htm
   Seamless access to dozens of databases including the content of
   OCLC's Electronic Collections Online.

67. **ProQuest**
   www.il.proquest.com/proquest/
   Online information service offering access to thousands of current
   periodicals and newspapers and containing full-text articles from
   1986 forward.

68. **ProQuest Historical Newspapers**
   www.il.proquest.com/proquest/histdemo/default.shtml
   New York Times, *Wall Street Journal*, and *Washington Post* dating
   back to the 19th century.

69. **ProQuest Newsstand**
   www.il.proquest.com/products/pt-product-newsstand.shtml
   Allows libraries to design custom databases from a digital newspaper
   archive, selecting from hundreds of dailies, including state, regional,
   national, and international titles.

70. *Reader's Guide to Periodical Literature*
   www.hwwilson.com/Databases/Readersg.htm
   H.W. Wilson's online and print indexing, abstracting, and full-text
   general interest magazine service.

71. **Roth LitFinder: Poem Finder, Story Finder, Essay Finder**
   www.litfinder.com/login.asp
   Index and access to full-text literature, explanations, images, and
   author biographies.

72. **SIRS Knowledge Source**
www.il.proquest.com/products/pt-product-SIRS-Knowledge-Source.shtml
Suite of highly selective full-text databases tied to curriculum.
Includes Renaissance (humanities), Government Reporter, Leading
Issues, and the general-interest SIRS Researcher.

73. **Wilson Omnifile Full Text Select**
www.hwwilson.com/dd/omnis_ft.htm
A multidisciplinary database of full-text periodical articles from
more than 1,600 titles.

74. **World Book Online Reference Center**
www.worldbookonline.com/wb/Login?ed=wb
Online version of the popular encyclopedia.

ASSOCIATIONS

75. **AASL (American Association of School Librarians)**
www.ala.org/ala/aasl/aaslindex.htm

76. **ACRL (Association of College and Research Libraries)**
www.ala.org/acrl

77. **American Dairy Association & Dairy Council Mid East**
www.adadcmideast.com/html/

78. **American Cancer Society**
www.cancer.org/

79. **CSLA (California School Library Association)**
www.schoolibrary.org/

80. **ISLMA (Illinois School Library Media Association)**
www.islma.org/

81. **OELMA (Ohio Educational Library Media Association)**
www.oelma.org/

GENERAL WEB SITES

82. **Ad*Access**
scriptorium.lib.duke.edu/adaccess
Duke University's database of more than 7,000 advertisements printed in U.S. and Canadian newspapers and magazines between 1911 and 1955.

83. **American Memory**
memory.loc.gov
Gateway to the rich primary source materials—more than 7 million digital items in more than 100 collections—held by the Library of Congress, relating to the history and culture of the United States.

84. **American Time Capsule: Three Centuries of Broadsides and Other Printed Ephemera**
memory.loc.gov/ammem/rbpehtml/pehome.html
A collection of more than 10,000 items including "proclamations, advertisements, blank forms, programs, election tickets, catalogs, clippings, timetables, and menus" from the American Revolution through the present day.

85. **AOL Members / AOL Hometown**
hometown.aol.com/
Free site hosting, journaling, and Web-design services provided by America Online.

86. **Apple Classrooms of Tomorrow (ACOT)**
www.apple.com/education/k12/leadership/acot/
Concluded in 1998, ACOT was a research and development collaboration among public schools, universities, research agencies, and Apple Computer, Inc.

87. **Ask a Librarian**
    www.loc.gov/rr/askalib/
    Online reference service provided by the Library of Congress.

88. **Big6**
    www.big6.com/
    Resource site for Eisenberg and Berkowitz's widely popular
    information literacy model.

89. **Blackboard**
    blackboard.com/
    Web-based platform for online course management.

90. **Cherished Keepsakes of 1904**
    www.ncsd.k12.mo.us/emints/mmueller/worldsfair
    webquest/indexworldsfairwq.html
    A social studies WebQuest designed for grades four through six that
    engages students in creating historical scrapbooks.

91. **Chico High School Library**
    dewey.chs.chico.k12.ca.us/
    Peter Milbury's award-winning high school site.

92. **Choose the Best Search for Your Information Need**
    www.noodletools.com/debbie/literacies/information/
    5locate/adviceengine.html
    Debbie Abilock's useful chart guides searchers through their options.

93. **Cohen, Laura: How to Choose a Search Engine or Directory**
    library.albany.edu/internet/choose.html
    Detailed chart linking to a wealth of appropriate choices from the
    University of Albany.

94. **Cohen, Laura: Second Generation Searching on the Web**
    library.albany.edu/internet/second.html
    Describes the innovative features of up-and-coming search tools (see
    "horizontal presentation of results").

95. **Cyberbee**
     www.cyberbee.com/
     Linda Joseph's rich site devoted to the wise and ethical integration of technology into curriculum; includes articles, online activities, treasure hunts, tips, annotated links, and research ideas.

96. **Cyberbee Copyright Tips**
     www.cyberbee.com/copyrt.html
     Linda Joseph's resource site for better understanding of copyright issues.

97. **Cyberbee Internet Safety Tips**
     www.cyberbee.com/safety.html
     Linda Joseph's advice and Web resource list.

98. **Dihydrogen Monoxide**
     www.dhmo.org/index.html
     Hoax site alerting us to the "controversy" surrounding the prevalent compound H_2O.

99. **Discovering American Memory**
     lcweb2.loc.gov/learn/educators/workshop/discover/
     Online workshop designed to introduce the American Memory collections through a series of activities for teachers and students. (*See also* **American Memory**).

100. **eBay**
     www.ebay.com/
     Hugely popular site for online shopping and bidding.

101. **Eisenberg, Michael**
     www.ischool.washington.edu/mbe/
     Dean of University of Washington Information School and co-creator of the Big6 model (*see separate reference for* **Big6***)* for information literacy.

102. Fair Use Guidelines for Educational Multimedia
www.libraries.psu.edu/mtss/fairuse/guidelines.html
This 1996 document provides educators and students with guidance in the ethical development and use of multimedia and other new technologies for educational purposes.

103. Friendster
friendster.com/
Network for connecting with old friends and finding new ones.

104. From Now On: The Research Cycle 2000
questioning.org/rcycle.html
Jamie McKenzie's online newsletter and rich article archive offer philosophy and practical tips for challenging student thinking and integrating thoughtful research into the curriculum.

105. Geocities
geocities.yahoo.com/
Free Web-hosting service and Web-design tools.

106. got books?
www.deblogan.com/gotbooks.html
Reading promotion program designed by Deb Logan.

107. Government Printing Office
www.gpoaccess.gov/
Search and ordering tool for the vast collection of publications of this U.S. federal agency.

108. Graphic Organizers
www.graphic.org/
Portal for concept mapping tools and information relating to their use with students.

109. Henry Hikes to Fitchburg and **Henry Builds a Cabin**
www.cyberbee.com/henryhikes/henry.html

Linda Joseph's creative online activities based on the book *Henry Hikes to Fitchburg* by D.B. Johnson.

110. IBM Community Relations
www.ibm.com/ibm/ibmgives/about/
A charitable arm of IBM, helping "people use information technology to improve the quality of life for themselves and others."

111. ICONnect
archive.ala.org/ICONN/whatis.html
This technology initiative of the American Association of School Librarians was designed to get students, library media specialists, and teachers connected to learning using the Internet.

112. ieSpell
www.iespell.com/
Spell-checker for Internet Explorer.

113. IMSA (Illinois Math and Science Academy) Information Fluency Project Portal
21cif.imsa.edu/
The 21st Century Information Fluency (21cif) Portal "provides news, information, tools, and standards-aligned instructional strategies for information literacy/fluency in K–16."

114. IMSA Fund for the Advancement of Education
www2.imsa.edu/giving/index.php
A not-for-profit corporation that accepts and distributes gifts and grants to support IMSA's mission and work.

115. IMSA Information Literacy Project Tips
21cif.imsa.edu/inform/tips
Tips for searching, evaluating, and integrating Internet content.

116. IMSA What is 21st Century Information Fluency?
21cif.imsa.edu/inform/program/whatisinfofluency.html

Description and three-dimensional model describing the components of digital information literacy.

117. **Inspiration**
www.inspiration.com/home.cfm
Popular and powerful concept mapping software.

118. **ISLMA Linking for Learning**
www.islma.org/resources.htm#linklearning
Connects Illinois school library programs to information literacy and state standards.

119. **Iwaynet**
www.iwaynet.net/
Internet access service serving central Ohio.

120. **JAKE (Jointly Administered Knowledge Environment)**
www.jake-db.org/docs/
Open source software project designed to make it easier for researchers to manage and access online journals and journal articles.

121. **KidsConnect**
archive.ala.org/ICONN/kcfavorites.html
Part of the technology initiative of the American Association of School Librarians, KidsConnect (temporarily suspended at this time) was an online question answering service run by school librarian volunteers.

122. **Lake Michigan Whale Watching**
www.classroomhelp.com/lessons/web/WHALES/
whale_in_MI.pdf
Hoax site "supporting" Lake Michigan whale and dolphin tourism.

123. **Library of Congress Subject Headings/Authorities**
authorities.loc.gov/

Free service that allows library staff to browse and display authority headings for subject, name, title, and name/title combinations, and to download authority records in MARC format.

124. LM_NET on the Web
www.eduref.org/lm_net/
The home page for the highly active LM_NET discussion group open to school library media specialists worldwide, and to others involved with the school library media field.

125. LMC Source
www.lmcsource.com/
Publisher of materials for library media specialists and distributor of Hi Willow Research and Publishing books.

126. LRS (Library Research Service)
www.lrs.org/index.asp
LRS generates library statistics and research for library professionals, educators, and the media. The site contains Keith Curry Lance's archive of research documenting relationships between school libraries and student achievement.

127. Lumpkin Foundation
www.lumpkinfoundation.org/
Private foundation that provides grants to nonprofits.

128. Massachusetts Recommended PreK-12 Instructional Technology Standards
www.doe.mass.edu/edtech/standards/itstand.pdf
Massachusetts state technology standards document.

129. Mayo Clinic
www.mayoclinic.com/
A rich and reliable site for information on healthy living, diseases and conditions, health calculators, and decision guidance.

130. **Mind Maps**
www.mind-map.com/EN/index.html
Home page for Tony Buzan's graphical concept mapping technique.

131. **Muse: The Metasearch Company**
www.museglobal.com/
Company creates customized federated search products for libraries.

132. **National Geographic**
www.nationalgeographic.com/
Rich Web site of the National Geographic Society includes learning activities, access to magazine, television, and film resources and an online store.

133. **National Zoo**
nationalzoo.si.edu/default.cfm
Web site of the National Zoo in Washington, DC.

134. **NETS for Students**
cnets.iste.org/
ISTE's (International Society for Technology in Education) National Educational Technology Standards for Students.

135. **Netscape Composer**
wp.netscape.com/communicator/composer/v4.0/
The popular browser's free HTML editor.

136. **NoodleTools (includes NoodleBib)**
www.noodletools.com/
Debbie and Damon Abilock's suite of interactive tools designed to aid students and professionals with online research. Includes tools for selecting a search engine, finding relevant sources, and citing sources in both MLA and APA style.

137. **Occupational Outlook Handbook**
www.bls.gov/oco/

Online version of the U.S. Bureau of Labor Statistics' survey of careers.

138. **OCLC Environmental Scan: Pattern Recognition**
www.oclc.org/membership/escan/default.htm
Online report presenting "a high-level view of the information landscape, intended both to inform and stimulate discussion about future strategic directions."

139. **Ohio's Guidelines for Effective School Library Media Programs**
www.ode.state.oh.us/Curriculum-Assessment/
school_library/
Ohio state standards document for library programs.

140. **Ohio's Technology Academic Content Standards**
www.ode.state.oh.us/academic_content_standards/
acstechnology.asp
Ohio state technology standards.

141. **Perry Network and the Center for the Study of Intellectual**
Development
www.perrynetwork.org/
Organization devoted to facilitating assessment, teaching, and learning related to William Perry's scheme of intellectual and ethical development.

142. **Pew Internet & American Life: Data Memo on Search Engines**
www.pewinternet.org/pdfs/PIP_Data_Memo_
Searchengines.pdf
Document examining the importance and popularity of search engines (Deborah Fallows, Lee Rainie, Graham Mudd).

143. **Polk Brothers Foundation**
www.polkbrosfdn.org/
Foundation devoted to offering grants to the low-income Chicago community.

144. **Revolutionary Viewpoints**
www.cyberbee.com/viewpoints/
Engaging learning activities created by Linda Joseph to enrich
students' reading of Howard Fast's *April Morning*.

145. **San Jose State University School of Library and**
Information Science
slisweb.sjsu.edu/
Graduate program for library science.

146. **SBC Foundation**
www.sbc.com/gen/corporate-citizenship?pid=2560
The philanthropic arm of this Fortune 50 telecommunications
company (formerly Ameritech) funds some educational programs.

147. **School Library Impact Studies**
www.lrs.org/impact.asp
Keith Curry Lance's work. *See also* **LRS**.

148. **Schrock, Kathy: Guide for Educators**
school.discovery.com/schrockguide/
Kathy maintains a major educational portal with her own original
content, as well as a categorized list of sites, to support the
curriculum and professional development.

149. **Search Engine Math**
searchenginewatch.com/facts/article.php/2156021
Danny Sullivan's basic search tips on how to use: +, –, "".

150. **Search Engine Watch**
searchenginewatch.com/
Comprehensive information about search engines—news, analysis,
marketing, searching, submission, reviews, ratings, and more.

151. **Sears Subject Headings**
www.hwwilson.com/print/searslst_18th.cfm

Ordering information for the basic list of subject headings long used by catalogers in small and medium-size libraries.

152. SEIR-TEC Internet Search Tool Quick Reference Guide
www.itrc.ucf.edu/iqr/
The SouthEast Initiatives Regional Technology in Education Consortium guide for determining which search engine to use and how to use it.

153. Simpson, Carol
www.unt.edu/slis/people/faculty/simpson.htm
Professor and copyright expert at University of North Texas School of Library and Information Science.

154. Smoking Gun
www.thesmokinggun.com/
Site offers "exclusive documents—cool, confidential, quirky—that can't be found elsewhere on the Web." Gathers much of its material from government and law enforcement sources.

155. Springfield Township High School Library KidSearch
mciu.org/~spjvweb/kidsearch.html
Leads elementary students to search tools on the free Web, online reference, and age-appropriate databases.

156. Springfield Township High School Library Pathfinders
mciu.org/~spjvweb/pathmenu.html
Joyce Valenza's guides for her students' major projects.

157. Spybot
www.spybot.info
Computer security software.

158. Student Learning Through Ohio School Libraries: The Ohio Research Study
www.oelma.org/studentlearning/default.asp

Offers empirical evidence related to how school libraries help students learn (Dr. Ross Todd and Dr. Carol Kuhlthau).

159. Tapped In

tappedin.org/tappedin/

An online workplace developed to serve an international community of education professionals.

160. ThinkQuest

www.thinkquest.org/

An international Web site–building competition, sponsored by the Oracle Education Foundation, that engages teams of students in creating and sharing educational sites.

161. U.S. Department of Education Fund for the Improvement of Education

www.ed.gov/programs/fie/index.html

This site describes the U.S. Department of Education's support of "Programs of National Significance" and "grants to state and local education agencies, nonprofit organizations, for-profit organizations, and other public and private entities that have been identified by the Congress in appropriations legislation."

162. W3 Consortium

www.w3.org/

Develops specifications, guidelines, software, and tools to optimize use of the Web.

163. Watch That Page

www.watchthatpage.com/

Service for automatically monitoring changes on selected Web pages.

164. WebQuest About Evaluating Web Sites

mciu.org/~spjvweb/evalwebstu.html

Joyce Valenza's activity asks teams of students to rank sites by consensus according to selected criteria.

165. **WebQuest Page**
webquest.sdsu.edu/
Bernie Dodge and Tom March's model for inquiry-oriented activities in which most or all of the information used by learners is drawn from the Web.

166. **Whodunit**
www.cyberbee.com/whodunnit/crime.html
Linda Joseph's online learning activities relating to forensic science.

JOURNALS

167. *American Libraries*
www.ala.org/alonline
Magazine of the American Library Association (ALA).

168. *Information Processing and Management*
www.sciencedirect.com/science/journal/03064573
International journal devoted to research in information science, computer science, cognitive science, and related areas.

169. *Information Searcher*
www.infosearcher.com/
Pam Berger's newsletter is the "longest published newsletter in K–12 education designed specifically for professionals working to integrate technology into the curriculum."

170. *Knowledge Quest*
www.ala.org/ala/aasl/aaslpubsandjournals/kqweb/
kqweb.htm
Bimonthly publication of the American Association of School Librarians (AASL). KQ's "articles address the integration of theory and practice in school librarianship and new developments."

171. *Library Media Connection*
www.linworth.com/
The Book Report and *Library Talk* are now both incorporated in

Library Media Connection, published by Linworth Publications. *LMC* offers articles, technology coverage, reviews, and more for library media specialists. *See* **LMC Source**.

172. *Media and Methods*
www.media-methods.com/
Technology and education magazine useful for making purchasing decisions.

173. *Multimedia & Internet @ Schools*
www.infotoday.com/MMSchools/default.shtml
A source of practical information for school librarians, technology specialists, and teachers on emerging education technology tools and their integration into curriculum (formerly *Multimedia Schools*).

174. *Ohio Media Spectrum*
www.oelma.org/
State journal for OELMA members (*see* **OELMA** *under Associations*).

175. *School Library Journal*
www.schoollibraryjournal.com/
Major resource for youth services librarians. Offers critical articles, archived reviews, and many special features.

176. *School Library Media Research: Refereed Research Journal of the AASL*
www.ala.org/aasl/SLMR/
An official research journal of the American Association of School Librarians (AASL); successor to *School Library Media Quarterly Online*.

177. *Science Magazine*
www.sciencemag.org/
Web-based home of *Science*, the global weekly of research.

178. *Science News*
    www.sciencenews.org/
    Weekly science newsmagazine covering the most important research in all fields of science in concise articles.

179. *Teacher Librarian*
    www.teacherlibrarian.com/
    Magazine for library professionals working with children and young adults, offers "articles exploring current issues such as collaboration, leadership, technology, advocacy, information literacy, and management."

BOOKS

180. Berger, Pam. *Internet for Active Learners: Curriculum-Based Strategies for K–12.* **Chicago: ALA, 1998.**
    www.alastore.ala.org
    Effective Internet integration strategies for library media specialists.

181. Berger, Pam. *21st Century Strategies for Strengthening Your School Library Program.* **Bellevue, WA: Bureau of Educational Research, 2004. (Handbook and Audiotape)**
    www.ber.org/CourseInfo.cfm?seid=BLB4F2-BOS
    Offers state-of-the-art "practical, ready-to-use ideas for making your library the heart of your school's instructional program."

182. Berger, Pam, and Susan Kinnell. *CD-ROM in Schools: A Directory and Practical Handbook for Media Specialists.* **Wilton, CT: Eight Bit Books, 1994.**
    Describes and reviews 300 CD-ROM titles.

183. Calishain, Tara. *Google Hacks: 100 Industrial-Strength Tips & Tools.* **Rael Dornfest, ed. Sebastopol, CA: O'Reilly, 2003.**
    oreilly.com/
    Tips and tricks for using Google in advanced, savvy ways.

184. Eisenberg, Michael B., and Robert E. Berkowitz. *Information Problem-Solving: The Big6 ™ Skills Approach to Library & Information Skills Instruction.* Norwood, NJ: Ablex, 1990. www.big6.com/

An in-depth investigation of the Big6 model and ideas for implementation. Includes instructional units and lessons.

185. Haycock, Ken, Michele Dober, and Barbara Edwards. *The Neal Schuman Authoritative Guide to Kids' Search Engines, Subject Directories, and Portals.* New York: Neal-Schuman, 2003. www.neal-schuman.com/

Analyzes free search engines, directories, and portals for grades 4–9.

186. *Information Power: Building Partnerships for Learning.* Chicago: American Library Association, 1998. www.alastore.ala.org/

AASL's national standards document for school library media programs.

187. Krashen, Stephen D. *The Power of Reading: Insights from the Research.* 2nd edition. Westport, CT: Libraries Unlimited, 2004. lu.com/

Krashen's research points to the effectiveness of free voluntary reading in increasing a child's ability to read, write, spell, and comprehend.

188. LeMay, Laura, and Arman Danesh. *Teach Yourself Web Publishing With HTML in a Week.* 4th edition. New York: Macmillan, 1997. www.mcp.com/

——. *Teach Yourself More Web Publishing With HTML in a Week.* Indianapolis: Sams, 1995. www.samspublishing.com/

Both titles were indispensable, practical guides for early Web developers.

189. Loertscher, David, and Blanche Woolls. *Information Literacy: A Review of the Research: A Guide for Practitioners and Researchers.* San Jose, CA: Hi Willow, 2001. Available through LMC Source. www.lmcsource.com/

Important compilation, synthesis, and analysis research critical to school librarians.

190. Logan, Debra Kay. *Information Skills Toolkit: Collaborative Integrated Instruction for the Middle Grades.* Worthington, OH: Linworth, 2000. www.linworth.com/

Detailed lessons, activity ideas, and assessments across the curriculum.

191. Logan, Debra Kay, and Cynthia Beueselink. *K–12 Web Pages: Planning and Publishing Excellent School Web Sites.* Worthington, OH: Linworth, 2002. www.linworth.com/

Practical ideas for beginning school Web developers.

192. Pappas, Marjorie L., and Ann E. Tepe. "Media, Visual, Technology and Information: A Comparison of Literacies." *Instructional Intervention for Information Use.* Ed. by Daniel Callison, Joy H. McGregor, and Ruth V. Small. San Jose, CA: Hi Willow Research and Publishing, 1998. Available through LMC Source. www.lmcsource.com/

Pappas and Tepe explore information literacy in a broader sense.

193. Pappas, Marjorie L., and Ann E. Tepe. *Pathways to Knowledge and Inquiry Learning.* Greenwood Village: Libraries Unlimited, 2002. lu.com/

Describes model for information literacy.

194. Perry, William G. *Forms of Ethical and Intellectual Development in the College Years.* San Francisco: Jossey-Bass, 1999. www.josseybass.com/WileyCDA/

Landmark book relating to student development research, based on Perry's research with Harvard undergraduates over a 15-year period.

195. **Schrock, Kathleen.** *Developing Web Pages for Educators.* **2nd edition. Westminster, CA: Teacher Created Materials, 2003. http://www.teachercreated.com/ kathyschrock.net/books.htm**
New edition takes teachers through developing a class Web page step-by-step.

196. **Schrock, Kathleen.** *Evaluating Internet Web Sites: An Educator's Guide.* **Manhattan, KS: The Master Teacher, 1997. www.masterteacher.com/ kathyschrock.net/books.htm**
The 32-page booklet provides educators with the tools needed to learn how to effectively evaluate a Web site.

197. **Schrock, Kathleen.** *Kathy Schrock's Every Day of the School Series.* **Worthington, OH: Linworth, 2002-2004. www.linworth.com/ kathyschrock.net/books.htm**
A series of books for educators that includes activities, tips, reproducibles, and much more.

198. **Schrock, Kathleen.** *Kathy's Slide Shows* **(CD-ROM). kathyschrock.net/books.htm**
Compiled from Kathy's presentations, in both PowerPoint and PDF formats.

199. **Schrock, Kathleen.** *Technology Connection: Building a Successful Library Media Program.* **Worthington, OH: Linworth, 2000. www.linworth.com/ kathyschrock.net/books.htm**
A compilation of useful technology articles from Linworth magazines.

200. Schrock, Kathleen, and Midge Frazel. *Inquiring Educators Want to Know: TeacherQuests for Today's Teachers.* Worthington, OH: Linworth, 2000.
www.linworth.com/
kathyschrock.net/books.htm
Questions and answers, offered in a framework called a TeacherQuest, for concerns that administrators, teachers, library media specialists, students, school board members, parents, and community members have in relation to technology in the schools.

201. Stripling, Barbara K., and Judy M. Pitts. *Brainstorms and Blueprints: Teaching Library Research as a Thinking Process.* Englewood, CO: Libraries Unlimited, 1988.
lu.com/
Classic work suggesting information literacy activities and theory for middle and high school.

202. *Super Searchers* series. Ed. Reva Basch. Information Today, Inc.
www.infotoday.com/supersearchers/
Each book in the series features interviews with 8–12 top online searchers in a specific discipline.

203. Valenza, Joyce Kasman. *Power Research Tools.* Chicago: ALA, 2002.
www.alastore.ala.org/
Organized into chapters relating to the information literacy standards, a collection of lessons, rubrics, graphic organizers, and curriculum designed to help students become more effective users of information.

204. Valenza, Joyce Kasman. *Power Tools: 100+ Essential Forms and Presentations for Your School Library Information Program.* Chicago: ALA, 1998. (out of print)
All the tools you need to organize, manage, teach, and collaborate as a teacher librarian.

205. Valenza, Joyce Kasman. *Power Tools Recharged.* Chicago: ALA, 2004.

www.alastore.ala.org/

Second edition of Power Tools, thoroughly revised to reflect changes in the information landscape.

JOURNAL ARTICLES AND PAPERS

206. Ebersole, Samuel E. *Adolescents' Use of the World-Wide Web in Ten Public Schools: A Uses and Gratifications Approach.*

faculty.colostate-pueblo.edu/samuel.ebersole/diss/

Ebersole's dissertation analyzes how public school students' attitudes and opinions toward the Web affect their use of Web materials in the school setting.

207. Kuhlthau, Carol C. "Information Search Process." SLMQ 18:1 (1998). *School Library Media Research.*

www.ala.org/ala/aasl/aaslpubsandjournals/slmrb/ editorschoiceb/infopower/selectkuhlthau2.htm

Summarizes five studies of students' perspectives on information seeking in response to a research assignment.

208. Loertscher, David. "All that Glitters May Not Be Gold." *Emergency Librarian* 24(2), 20–21, 23–25, 1996.

Argues that students need to spend a great deal of time consuming the information they find. Too many do not feel they should spend time consuming information—reading, viewing, listening, thinking—and instead rush toward product creation.

209. Stripling, Barbara K. "Fostering Literacy and Inquiry." *School Library Journal*, 1 Sept. 2003, 49(9): S5.

www.schoollibraryjournal.com/article/CA319394.html

Stripling outlines an information literacy process—connect, wonder, investigate, construct, express, reflect.

210. **"Surfing made easy."** *NEA Today*, **Dec 1995, 14(5): 25.**
The National Education Association (NEA) newsletter article that "discovered" Kathy Schrock.

211. **Whelan, Debra Lau. "13,000 Kids Can't Be Wrong."** *School Library Journal*, **50:2 (Feb. 2004): 46–50.**
www.schoollibraryjournal.com/article/CA377858.html
Article reports on the Ohio study, Student Learning Through Ohio School Libraries, which revealed that an overwhelming number of students believe that school libraries help them become better learners.

About the Author

Joyce Valenza is librarian at Springfield Township High School in Pennsylvania. She is the *techlife@school* columnist for the *Philadelphia Inquirer* and author of two previous books, *Power Research Tools* and *Power Tools Recharged*. Her video series, Internet Searching Skills, was a YALSA (Young Adult Library Services Association) Selected Video for Young Adults in 1999. Another video series, Library Skills for Children, was released in 2003, and a six-volume video series, Research Skills for Students, was released in fall 2004. Joyce's Virtual Library won the IASL (International Association of School Librarianship) School Library Web Page of the Year Award for 2001.

Joyce is active in the American Library Association (ALA), the American Association of School Librarians (AASL), YALSA, and the International Society for Technology in Education (ISTE). She contributes regularly to *Classroom Connect*, *VOYA*, *Learning and Leading with Technology*, and *School Library Journal*. Joyce speaks nationally about issues relating to libraries and thoughtful use of educational technology. She is a Milken Educator and an American Memory Fellow, and is currently working on a doctoral degree at the University of North Texas.

Joyce lives—and shares workstations—with her husband and two nearly adult children in Rydal, Pennsylvania. At the conclusion of her doctoral program, she may return to her hobbies of reading, creating Web sites, dancing, crafting, shopping, enjoying wine, and sleeping.

Joyce's Virtual Library is located at mciu.org/~spjvweb
Her home page: mciu.org/~spjvweb/jvweb.html
Her professional site: neverendingsearch.com

About the Editor

Reva Basch, executive editor of the Super Searcher series, has written four books of her own: *Researching Online For Dummies* (2nd edition with Mary Ellen Bates, Hungry Minds, Inc.), *Secrets of the Super Net Searchers* (Information Today, Inc.), *Secrets of the Super Searchers* (Information Today, Inc.), and *Electronic Information Delivery: Evaluating Quality and Value* (Gower). She has edited and contributed chapters, introductions, and interviews to several books about the Internet and online information retrieval. She was the subject of a profile in *Wired* magazine, which called her "the ultimate intelligent agent."

Prior to starting her own business in 1986, Reva was Vice President and Director of Research at Information on Demand, a pioneering independent research company. She has designed front-end search software for major online services, written and consulted on technical, marketing, and training issues for both online services and database producers, and published extensively in information industry journals. She has keynoted at international conferences in Australia, Scandinavia, Europe, and the U.K., as well as North America.

Reva is a Past-President of the Association of Independent Information Professionals. She has a degree in English literature, *summa cum laude*, from the University of Pennsylvania, and a master's degree in library science from the University of California, Berkeley. She began her career as a corporate librarian, ran her own independent research business for 10 years, and has been online since the mid-1970s. She lives in northern California with her husband and several excellent cats.

Index

M

More Great Books from Information Today, Inc.

Yahoo! to the Max
An Extreme Searcher Guide

By Randolph Hock
Foreword by Mary Ellen Bates

"We review many new publications, good or not so good, but we know straight away that if it's a Ran Hock title then it's going to be great." —William Hann, FreePint

With its many and diverse features, it's not easy for any individual to keep up with all that Yahoo! has to offer. Fortunately, Randolph (Ran) Hock—"The Extreme Searcher"—has created a reader-friendly guide to his favorite Yahoo! tools for research, communication, investment, e-commerce, and a range of other useful activities. In *Yahoo! to the Max*, Ran provides background, techniques, and tips designed to help Web users take advantage of many of Yahoo!'s most valuable offerings— from its portal features, to Yahoo! Groups, to unique tools some users have yet to discover. The author's regularly updated Web page helps readers stay current on the new and improved Yahoo! features he recommends.

256 pp/softbound/ISBN 0-910965-69-2 • $24.95

The Web Library
Building a World Class Personal Library with Free Web Resources

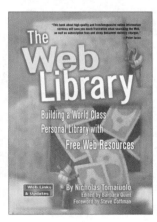

By Nicholas G. Tomaiuolo
Edited by Barbara Quint

With this remarkable, eye-opening book and its companion Web site, Nicholas G. (Nick) Tomaiuolo shows how anyone can create a comprehensive personal library using no-cost Web resources. If you were to calculate the expense of purchasing the hundreds of print and fee-based electronic publications that are available for free with "The Web Library," you'd quickly recognize the potential of this book to save you thousands, if not millions, of dollars (fortunately, Nick does the calculating for you!). This is an easy-to-use guide, with chapters organized into sections corresponding to departments in a physical library. *The Web Library* provides a wealth of URLs and examples of free material you can start using right away, but, best of all, it offers techniques for finding and collecting new content as the Web evolves. Start building your personal Web library today!

440 pp/softbound/ISBN 0-910965-67-6 • $29.95

Net Effects
How Librarians Can Manage the Unintended Consequences of the Internet

Edited by Marylaine Block

The Internet is a mixed blessing for libraries and librarians. On the one hand, it provides opportunities to add services and expand collections; on the other, it has increased user expectations and contributed to techno stress. Today, the Net is challenging librarians' ability to select, threatening the survival of the book, necessitating continuous retraining, presenting new problems of access and preservation, putting new demands on budgets, and embroiling information professionals in legal controversies.

In *Net Effects*, librarian, journalist, and Internet guru Marylaine Block examines the issues and brings together a wealth of insights, war stories, and solutions. Nearly 50 articles by dozens of imaginative librarians—expertly selected, annotated, and integrated by the editor—suggest practical and creative ways to deal with the range of Internet "side effects," regain control of the library, and avoid being blindsided by technology again.

380 pp/hardbound/ISBN 1-57387-171-0 • $39.50

Super Searcher, Author, Scribe
Successful Writers Share Their Internet Research Secrets

By Loraine Page
Edited by Reva Basch

The impact of the Internet on the writing profession is unprecedented, even revolutionary. Wired writers of the 21st century rely on the Web to do research, to collaborate, to reach out to readers, and even to publish and sell their work.

Super Searcher, Author, Scribe illuminates the state of the art, bringing together a broad range of successful, Web-savvy writers to share their tips, techniques, sites, sources, and success stories. *Link-Up* editor Loraine Page combines a deft interviewing style and knowledge of the craft of writing to draw out gems of wisdom from 15 leading journalists, book authors, writing instructors, and professional researchers in the literary field.

216 pp/softbound/ISBN 0-910965-58-7 • $24.95

The Extreme Searcher's Internet Handbook
A Guide for the Serious Searcher

By Randolph Hock

The Extreme Searcher's Internet Handbook is the essential guide for anyone who uses the Internet for research—librarians, teachers, students, writers, business professionals, and others who need to search the Web proficiently. Award-winning writer and Internet trainer Randolph "Ran" Hock covers strategies and tools (including search engines, directories, and portals) for all major areas of Internet content.

There's something here for every Internet searcher. Readers with little to moderate searching experience will appreciate the helpful, easy-to-follow advice, while experienced searchers will discover a wealth of new ideas, techniques, and resources. Anyone who teaches the Internet will find this book indispensable.

As a reader bonus, the author maintains "The Extreme Searcher's Web Page" featuring links, updates, news, and much more. It's the ideal starting place for any Web search.

296 pp/softbound/ISBN 0-910965-68-4 • $24.95

Best Technology Practices in Higher Education

Edited by Les Lloyd

A handful of progressive teachers and administrators are integrating technology in new and creative ways at their colleges and universities, raising the bar for all schools. In his latest book, editor Les Lloyd (*Teaching with Technology*) has sought out the most innovative and practical examples in a range of key application areas, bringing together more than 30 technology leaders to share their success stories. The book's 18 chapters include firsthand accounts of school technology projects that have transformed classrooms, services, and administrative operations. The four major sections are "Best Practices in Teaching and Course Delivery," "Best Practices in Administrative Operations," "Technical or Integrative Best Practices," and "Future Best Practices."

Best Technology Practices in Higher Education is an invaluable resource for technology and information staff, and for provosts and presidents who need to gauge how their schools stack up and to challenge staff to embrace the best that new technology has to offer.

256 pp/hardbound/ISBN 1-57387-208-3 • $39.50

The Accidental Library Manager

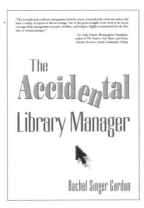

By Rachel Singer Gordon

Most librarians enter the field intending to focus on a particular specialty, but eventually need to take on certain supervisory or managerial responsibilities in order to move forward. In *The Accidental Library Manager*, author Rachel Singer Gordon provides support and background for new managers, aspiring managers, and those who find themselves in unexpected management roles. Gordon fills in the gaps left by brief and overly theoretical library school coursework, showing library managers how to be more effective in their positions and how to think about their work in terms of the goals of their larger institutions. Included are insights from working library managers at different levels and in various types of libraries, addressing a wide range of management issues and situations. Not to be missed: comments from library staff about the qualities they appreciate—and the styles and attitudes they find counterproductive—in their own bosses. This readable and reassuring guide is a must for any librarian who wishes to succeed in a management position.

368 pp/softbound/ISBN 1-57387-210-5 • $29.50

The Accidental Webmaster

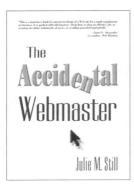

By Julie M. Still

Here is a lifeline for the individual who has not been trained as a Webmaster, but who—whether by choice or under duress—has become one nonetheless. While most Webmastering books focus on programming and related technical issues, *The Accidental Webmaster* helps readers deal with the full range of challenges they face on the job. Author, librarian, and accidental Webmaster Julie Still offers advice on getting started, setting policies, working with ISPs, designing home pages, selecting content, drawing site traffic, gaining user feedback, fundraising, avoiding copyright problems, and much more.

208 pp/softbound/ISBN 1-57387-164-8 • $29.50